Life of Riley: A Marriage Therapist's New Approach

by

Timothy J. McCarthy, PhD

TELEMACHUS PRESS

Life of Riley: A Marriage Therapist's New Approach
Copyright © 2025 Timothy J. McCarthy, PhD
All rights reserved. No part of this book may be reproduced, transmitted, downloaded, decompiled, stored in any retrieval system, or translated in any form, or by any means, whether electronic or mechanical without permission in writing from the author.

The publisher does not have any control over and does not assume any responsibility for author or third-party websites or their content.

Cover Design by Telemachus Press, LLC

Cover art:
Copyright ©iStockPhoto/1295736084/Kseniya Lapteva

Visit the author website:
http://www.relationshipcocoaching.com

Softly Specific Co-Coaching℠ is a service mark of Timothy J. McCarthy, PhD

ISBN: 978-1-965121-06-1 (eBook)
ISBN: 978-1-965121-05-4 (Paperback)

Version 2025.03.20

Praise for Life of Riley

"This book is unique; both educational and engaging, dissimilar fictional couples struggle with their romantic and family bonds but interspersed in each narrative are insights from a skilled marital and family therapist coping with his own relationships, yet tutoring about a new method of conflict management with growing clarity from chapter to chapter.

The narrative and the coaching are seamlessly woven into a tapestry you don't see coming. Couples are introduced intertwined with one another, across generations, hooking the reader to care for each individual, while also learning to recognize, examine and improve their interpersonal thoughts and feelings that feed conflict.

You will care about the people, you will care about their connections, and while immersed in the story you will easily learn an emerging technique to reduce conflict in loving relationships.

If a romantic novel and a clinical text produced a love child, it would be Life of Riley."

—**John C. Linton**, PhD, ABPP, HSP-P
Emeritus Professor of Behavioral Medicine and Dean
West Virginia University School of Medicine, Charleston West Va.

"In his latest novel, Mr. McCarthy skillfully captures the complexities and challenges faced by couples in modern life. Through the dynamics of the various couples portrayed, McCarthy demonstrates a deep understanding of the ways couples can drift toward disconnection and resentment.

What sets this novel apart is that it doesn't just illustrate the difficulties of maintaining healthy relationships—it offers practical strategies for navigating conflict and fostering stronger bonds. The novel is not only a compelling story but also a valuable resource for readers seeking to better understand relationships.

For those turned off by the conventional self-help genre, this book presents a refreshing blend of storytelling and insight, making it an engaging and informative read for anyone interested in personal and relational growth."

—**Christine Hunter**, MA.LP.
Mn Couples Therapy Center
Roseville Mn.

"In his new book, 'The Life of Riley', Dr Tim McCarthy starts with the observation, sadly true, that 'we live in a society that is socially underdeveloped, especially in how to succeed in romantic relationships'. We are under trained for love and it is a training we sorely need. One of our society's biggest expressed desires is for a lifelong loving partnership, yet failure rates remain stubbornly high. Research in the past 30 years has provided important information about what is needed to fulfill this longing. We need to know this information, and also know how to apply it in our lives. Dr. McCarthy makes the effort to illustrate both of these steps in an accessible way through stories of 4 couples who work to integrate the science of love into their lives."

—**Bryan Kingsriter**, LMFT
MN Couples Therapy Center

Preface

The Life of Riley isn't your ordinary relationship advice book. Instead, it's an entertaining and insightful story about a new very different approach to relationships.

We live in a society that is socially underdeveloped. We may be technologically and materially advanced, however, we have failed to provide any real widespread education or training in how to be successful in romantic relationships and marriage.

After thirty-six years as a PhD psychologist and licensed Marriage and Family therapist, it has become overwhelmingly evident to me that if couples simply were better educated, they could avoid many problems or at least be better able to expect the kinds of issues that so commonly occur in relationships. And they could more quickly initiate seeing a marriage therapist at a much earlier point in time; proactively getting needed help to avoid the unnecessary onset of more serious problems.

Research shows that couples take on the average six years before seeking a marriage therapist to help solve their problems. Think of how ridiculous that is, would you wait six years to fix a problem with your car? What shape would your car be in after 6 years?

So many hard-working busy couples out there have become accustomed to accepting a level of relationship happiness and satisfaction far less than what they really would like. Society sadly reinforces this lower bar through a variety of very harmful culturally driven self-limiting beliefs such as "this is to be expected, it's the reality of marriage, it's not all romance and roses, don't ask your partner to change just accept them the way they are, etc."

As a result of this couples tend to just go on "cruise control." They forget about achieving a deeper love connection and a higher quality of relationship. If only all these couples could just be better educated and encouraged to challenge their own complacency. They could have a much happier and more satisfying relationship even without making all that much effort. Thus, the impetus for this book.

The objective of *The Life of Riley* is not just to help couples who have more serious problems that might lead to marriage therapy. It is meant for the much broader audience of all who are in a romantic relationship. The focus is on a topic resonating with most every adult reader. That is: the inevitable reality of expected problems and issues bound to occur <u>for all of us</u> in romantic relationships and marriage. But even more importantly how we can overcome the traps and pitfalls pre-destined to occur using this new approach to relationship-marriage success.

Through the lens of the Rileys, a colorful fictional family guided by marriage expert Dr. Steve Riley, you can expect to learn small and big ways to make changes in your relationships that will take you out of cruise control. The lessons are imparted through real circumstances, as Dr. Riley's two adult children and their respective partners encounter universally common relationship problems and learn how to successfully overcome them using the principles of this new approach.

Radical social change is really needed for better educating couples. Some day, society will wake up and devote the attention needed to this issue. Until then let this be an interesting and entertaining fictional story for people like you looking for something good to read which also opens your eyes to new relationship insights.

So, settle back now and see what is about to happen with Dr. Steve Riley and his family. Enjoy their story and learn what you can from their experiences. And if you feel inspired, take your own relationship to an even deeper level of love and the very highest level of satisfaction possible!

Acknowledgments

I would like to give special appreciation to all the couples that I have worked with who opened their hearts and minds to each other while diligently applying the best practice principles being conveyed in this book. Their hard work serves as proof for how couples can truly change themselves and their relationships.

In addition, I greatly appreciate the time taken by other colleagues and therapists who reviewed this book and have expressed such positive endorsement of it:

John Linton, PhD; Christine Hunter, MA, LP; and Bryon Kingsriter, MA, LMFT.

May the future bring much greater social awareness in our society for the need to educate all couples in achieving their highest level of love and satisfaction in their relationships through using these relationship best practices!

Contents

Life of Riley: A Marriage Therapist's New Approach

Introduction

Life of Riley: A Marriage
Therapist's New Approach

The Life of Riley isn't your ordinary relationship advice book. Instead, it's an entertaining and insightful story about a new very different approach to relationships.

We live in a society that is socially underdeveloped. We may be technologically and materially advanced, however, we have failed to provide any real widespread education or training in how to be successful in romantic relationships and marriage.

With over thirty-six years as a PhD psychologist and licensed Marriage and Family therapist, it has become overwhelmingly evident to me that if couples simply were better educated, they could avoid many problems or at least be better able to expect the kinds of issues that so commonly occur in relationships. And they could more quickly initiate seeing a marriage therapist at a much earlier point in time; proactively getting needed help to avoid the unnecessary onset of more serious problems.

Research shows that couples take on the average six years before seeking a marriage therapist to help solve their problems. Think of how ridiculous that is, would you wait six years to fix a problem with your car? What shape would your car be in after 6 years?

So many hard-working busy couples out there have become accustomed to accepting a level of relationship happiness and satisfaction far less than what they really would like. Society sadly reinforces this lower bar through a variety of very harmful culturally driven self-limiting beliefs such as "this is to be expected, it's the reality of marriage, it's not all romance and roses, don't ask your partner to change just accept them the way they are, etc."

As a result of this couples tend to just go on "cruise control." They forget about achieving a deeper love connection and a higher quality of relationship. If only all these couples could just be better educated and encouraged to challenge their own complacency. They could have a much happier and more satisfying relationship even without making all that much effort. Thus, the impetus for this book.

The objective of *The Life of Riley* is not just to help couples who have more serious problems that might lead to marriage therapy. It is meant for the much broader audience of all who are in a romantic relationship. The focus is on a topic resonating with most every adult reader. That is: the inevitable reality of expected problems and issues bound to occur <u>for all of us</u> in romantic relationships and marriage. But even more importantly how we can overcome the traps and pitfalls pre-destined to occur using this new approach to relationship-marriage success.

Through the lens of the Rileys, a colorful fictional family guided by marriage expert Dr. Steve Riley, you can expect to learn small and big ways to make changes in your relationships that will take you out of cruise control. The lessons are imparted through real circumstances, as Dr. Riley's two adult children and their respective partners encounter universally common relationship problems and learn how to successfully overcome them using the principles of this new approach.

Radical social change is really needed for better educating couples. Some day, society will wake up and devote the attention needed to this issue. Until then let this be an interesting and entertaining fictional story for people like you looking for something good to read which also opens your eyes to new relationship insights.

So, settle back now and see what is about to happen with Dr. Steve Riley and his family. Enjoy their story and learn what you can from their experiences. And if you feel inspired, take your own relationship to an even deeper level of love and the very highest level of satisfaction possible!

Dr. Riley's podcast is coming to you now. His voice begins and so does our story...

"Every relationship goes through two stages. First, there is an initial honeymoon stage. Everything feels wonderful. Being in love, ah so incredible!

Then, after some time passes the true reality of relationship challenges are encountered. It's there we must move into the second phase where the real work begins. Are you ready to walk this journey together and learn how to achieve a truly extraordinary relationship?"

Part 1:
The Riley Family Enters the Fun Honeymoon Reunion Phase

Chapter 1

Podcast #1
Relationship Co-Coaching: A New Approach to Deeper Love, Less Conflict

---

"This is Dr. Steve Riley—I'm pleased you are listening to this podcast today and are considering new ideas for how to improve your relationship. You will learn new insights and tools to help you achieve the highest possible happiness in your relationship. A new model for relationships is offered here, one that will challenge your thinking. If it succeeds, this approach may change some of the core beliefs you have accepted, either consciously or subconsciously about romantic relationships, love, and marriage.

Relationship Co-Coaching will help you break through negative behavior patterns and learn new, positive ones. And it will encourage you and your partner to unselfishly go out of the way to help each other feel deeply loved at the core of your being in the exact ways you both need."

Heather and Daniel Green sat on Dr. Steve Riley's brown leather couch in a quaint building outside of Minneapolis ready to discuss their marriage. They had both heard his podcast, but more than that they believed he could help them.

Dr. Steve Riley was a highly regarded marriage and family therapist in the greater Minneapolis area quickly becoming known for his new, very different approach. The Greens had found him after Heather saw a news segment on the local channel covering the release of Dr. Riley's book "Relationship Co-Coaching: A New Approach to Deeper Love, Less Conflict" and his corresponding podcast. After the segment aired, Heather immediately picked up her phone, did a quick Google search and found the direct line to Dr. Riley's office. Within five minutes, she'd booked their appointment and now here they sat discussing their biggest problem.

"We're just not like we used to be," Heather Green sighed without even looking at her husband Daniel.

"It's not that bad," Daniel said defensively as he turned to face her.

"But it's not great," Heather replied then looked at Dr. Riley for guidance. Her big green eyes said everything—she was frustrated. Dr. Steve Riley knew exactly what was going on. He'd seen it before.

Heather and Daniel Green were the epitome of the typical couple Dr. Riley saw in his practice. Happy on the outside but struggling behind closed doors. They weren't always like this. When they first started dating in their early thirties, they were full of vigor for life and love. She, a red-headed go-getter, he, the child of a Texan father and a second-generation Chinese mother were both busy with their careers yet still found time to nurture their budding relationship. Heather had recently been promoted to Director of Communications at a small food company that delivered organic goods to busy moms. The architecture firm Daniel worked for had started to trust him to take lead on some of their biggest projects. Despite their busyness, they spent nearly every weekend together, exploring all that the bustling city of Minneapolis had to offer.

Now, twelve years, three kids and a move to the suburbs later their relationship had dwindled to transactional exchanges of *pick up the kids from here, drop them off there, work was fine, can you order dinner?*

"I don't know what happened," Heather exclaimed. "We were so good together in the beginning."

"We really were," Daniel added fondly.

Dr. Riley could see the hurt in both of their eyes. "You know it's not your fault, right?" he said.

"That's not what the last three therapists told us," Daniel retorted.

"That may be true, but I have a different perspective," Dr. Riley said then continued on, "Our society is set up against you."

"How?" Daniel asked. From everything he'd been told, it was his fault that his marriage was on shaky ground. What did society have to do with it?

"Think about it. We work so hard to get ahead in our careers, to buy the house and take the nice vacations and not only are we rewarded for all that work, but we're given feedback to improve and we're encouraged the entire way."

"That's true, but so?" Daniel replied as Heather glared at him with a *let him finish* stare.

"The opposite is true for our relationships," Dr. Riley continued. "There is no training for marriage. Yet, we still expect people to fall in love, get married, have kids and live happily ever after. We send them out into the abyss and say good luck with no coaching at all."

"That's so true," Heather said as Daniel flicked at a piece of lint on his designer jeans.

"Let me ask you this," Dr. Riley started again. "When your daughter turns sixteen are you going to buy the fancy car she's been obsessing over, hand her the keys and say good luck out there? Of course not. You're going to send her to driver's ed. You're going to take her out on test drives and coach her through the process. You're going to advise her on what to do in every situation. You're going to research cars and make sure that what she drives is safe. I want you to look at marriage counseling in the same way."

"Like driver's ed?" Daniel asked with a piqued interest.

"I guess like that," Dr. Riley replied with a laugh. He'd never heard his practice compared to a teenage rite of passage, but it made sense.

"If this is true, they should really have relationship class in school," Heather added.

"You're preaching to the choir, my friend," Dr. Riley started. "I've been doing this for over thirty years now and it still upsets me that even though the divorce rate for new couples is 40-50 percent, nothing is being done about it. You two are both successful. Could you imagine accepting a job where your prospective boss tells you that your chances of achieving success are about 50 percent and there's an equal chance you'll fail and be fired?"

"Absolutely not," Daniel stated.

"No way," Heather replied.

"This is why I'm so passionate about helping couples like you. I want to give you that fighting chance. You've done nothing wrong here. It's not your fault that our society is primed to praise material success. And it's not your fault that there's a complete lack of education and training for how to be successful in romantic relationships."

Dr. Riley watched as Heather and Daniel both relaxed into the couch. He smiled at the sight. It was the same sight he saw every time his couples realized they weren't to blame for all their problems.

"So, this is fixable?" Heather asked.

"Absolutely," the doctor said with complete certainty. Heather relaxed even further into the couch. Her diamond ring caught a ray of sun and reflected onto the wall behind Daniel.

"Okay, so, what do we do now?" Heather asked enthusiastically.

"Well, it's time to learn all the things you never learned. I guess you can look at it a little bit like going back to school."

Heather appeared apprehensive. "I tried to learn French last year, and I was awful at it."

"It's hard to teach an old dog new tricks," Daniel commented. Heather turned and glared at him. "I meant me," Daniel covered.

"Are we doomed?" Heather asked.

"You're not doomed," Dr. Riley said. "In fact, I'd say at this point you're primed for success because you've taken the first step in showing up here together."

"When you put it that way, I feel a lot better," Daniel said as he looked over at his wife and asked, "Do you?" Heather smiled at him for the first time since they'd walked into Dr. Riley's office.

Though things had been rough for them lately they missed the way they used to be. They missed spontaneous road trips, the coming home to a surprise champagne dinner, the being able to relax on the couch without walking on eggshells.

"This all sounds great. But how? We've tried therapy before. We've learned the communication tricks and we're usually good for about two weeks, then you know what happens? It all goes back to the way it was before. She's nagging, I'm frustrated, and it just keeps going."

"Daniel," Heather blurted.

"What? I'm being honest," Daniel said with a shrug.

"See what I have to deal with?" Heather said with a scoff. "Two seconds ago, we were smiling and now we're back to this."

The tension in the room rose as Daniel thought about his retort. But before he could say anything, Dr. Riley stepped in. "Okay, okay look. Let's pause for a minute and reflect. Do you both love each other?"

"Of course," Heather said.

"Yes," Daniel replied.

"Then that's where we're starting. Let's put all the other issues aside for a moment. I want you to turn and look at each other."

Daniel and Heather turned their bodies to face one another on the couch.

"Now grab hands and look in each other's eyes and think about the best moment you had together."

There was a long pause, then both their faces lit up.

"St. Martin, second day of our honeymoon, Happy Bay," Daniel stated with the biggest grin.

Heather started to blush then added, "Remember that little secluded spot behind the mangrove tree?"

"I don't need to know all the details," Dr. Riley said cutting her off. "But I want you to remember this moment and come back to it when you need to."

Dr. Riley watched as they continued to happily gaze at each other. He found joy in pushing two people who loved each other to a point where they could pause and remember who they used to be. Heather and Daniel squeezed each other's hands. Their defenses were softened and the spark between them was still alive.

"I knew there was a very deep, special love still alive there. Are you ready to return to it?" Dr. Riley asked.

Both Heather and Daniel nodded enthusiastically as Dr. Riley concluded their session. "We're going to get through this together and when you finish you will have discovered that relationship co-coaching can lead to a renewed love where both of you feel truly happy and deeply loved in the marriage."

The thought of a renewed love made Heather smile. As they gathered their belongings Daniel started a little small talk. "Do you have kids, Dr. Riley?"

"Two, but they're grown and flown," Dr. Riley replied.

"That must be nice. I can't wait for the day."

"Yeah, but don't rush through the moments of them being young. You'll miss it when you're my age."

"Really?" Heather asked. She already knew that when they returned home the house would be complete chaos and she wasn't exactly looking forward to it.

"Most of it. But being an empty nester is pretty great too. There's something satisfying and life enhancing about knowing your kids are successful and happy without you."

"One day we'll be there, honey," Daniel said as they walked out the door hand in hand. "And it'll be as great as Dr. Riley says."

"I hope so," Heather replied.

~~~

After his session with the Greens, Dr. Riley headed straight to Humble Luxury to meet with Anna Williams, his realtor. He was always on a high after the first session with a new couple went well, but that day he felt even more elated.

For the last ten years, Dr. Riley had had his sight set on owning a place on the water. Last summer, after he and his wife Kulap, whose family originated from Singapore, were invited out on a friend's boat for the Fourth of July, Dr. Riley had decided that Humble Lake would be the ultimate place to live.

"I could see us here in a year," Kulap had said as they sat anchored in the middle of the lake, fireworks exploding triumphantly above them.

"Me too," Dr. Riley had replied. The house that sat directly in front of them was lit up. A BBQ took place in the backyard. Little kids ran around with sparklers, teens sat on the dock dipping their toes in the water. The adults sipped beer and wine in the chaise loungers that had been scattered around the perfectly manicured lawn.

Although Dr. Riley's kids were all gone, he could picture he and Kulap sitting in their matching outdoor recliners reading the paper and sipping coffee as the sun rose every morning. At night, they'd grab a glass of wine and sit near the edge of the water and watch the sun set, and eventually when his kids, yes, *his* kids were more settled into their lives and had kids of their own he'd teach them how to swim and throw BBQs himself. Until then, it would be he and Kulap living out their empty nester life.

The thought on that Independence Day was a beautiful one until Dr. Riley felt a pang of guilt over his future with Kulap. On the water that night, he felt bad because he knew that what he was really dreaming of was the future that he and his first wife Emily had planned long ago when the kids were still in diapers. Though he wanted all those things with Kulap, he still had moments of pain. Emily had passed six years prior and though she had told him that it was her wish for him to move on and find happiness when she was gone, the memory of her and the plans they had had were still bittersweet.

Kulap and Dr. Riley had a wonderful marriage but that didn't mean his memory of Emily would ever fully disappear. She would always be in his heart and he felt blessed to be truly happy and deeply loved. So, when Kulap couldn't stop talking about their night on the boat and a future in a lake house Dr. Riley made it his mission to make it happen.

He poured his heart and soul into his book and his practice and his podcast, tasked Kulap with making the condo they lived in saleable and worked with his financial advisor to ensure that they would still be able to retire in ten years. The advisor had said they'd be perfectly set, then joked, "so long as your kids don't move back in with you and suck you dry." Kulap and Dr. Riley had laughed, that was impossible.

Dr. Riley's kids were completely independent, doing their own thing. Kevin, his youngest at twenty-seven, had been married a year and he and his wife were focused on creating careers that they would both be passionate about for years to come. His eldest, Nola, was twenty-nine and working on a career as an actress in Los Angeles. Her hard work had started to pay off and she had finally started to book consistent gigs. In fact, she'd just done a pilot episode for a new TV series that would hopefully make it to air.

Dr. Riley had no concerns about his kids. Everything was as it should be, and he was excited for this day.

Outside the office of Humble Luxury, Dr. Riley met up with Kulap and together they walked inside to sign the final paperwork on their dream home.

After twenty minutes of going through all the financials, putting their signatures on a gazillion different documents and asking all the necessary questions, the dream was finally theirs.

"Congratulations! You are now the proud owners of the house at 95 Larch," Anna the realtor said as she handed over the keys.

Dr. Riley enthusiastically took them into his hands and immediately added them to the leather keyring his kids had made for him at sleepaway camp nearly twenty years ago. It was weathered and worn but it was the perfect reminder of the incredible family he had.

Kulap gave Dr. Riley a hug and a long kiss that bordered on inappropriate but was still acceptable. Anna took it as a sign that Dr. Riley was a man who not only talked the talk but walked the walk. This made Anna happy.

"One more thing," Anna said as she walked the Rileys toward the door. "I've been meaning to thank you."

"For what?" Dr. Riley asked.

"For your book," Anna replied. "I'm sure you get this all the time, but it really made a huge difference in my marriage."

"He does hear it all the time, but he loves it," Kulap retorted. Dr. Riley gave Anna a sheepish smile. There was an awkward pause until Kulap continued. "Go on, tell him. Every woman's got a story."

Anna paused, unsure if she should proceed.

"It's okay," Dr. Riley said. "I love hearing what's worked for couples."

Kulap nodded in agreement and Anna softly began.

"Well, you see, over the last couple years I've been really busy growing this business."

"And you've done a fantastic job helping us get the house we wanted," Dr. Riley added.

"Thank you. But that wasn't the problem. I knew my husband desperately wanted us to spend more time together, but I just couldn't figure out how to make it work. And, honestly, I didn't think I had to. This was my second chance at a career. I gave up my first one to stay home with the kids, so I felt like he owed this time to me. He got his shot, why couldn't I have mine?"

"You go girl," Kulap said as she held up her right hand for a high-five. Anna gently tapped her palm to Kulap's.

"Anyway, it wasn't until I read your book that I really saw how much fulfilling your partner's Love Needs was a huge part of a good relationship. When I finally listened and empathized with his needs, I started to make more time for him. And you know what? Not only did our relationship improve, but so did my business because I was genuinely happy," Anna finished with a smile.

"I'm glad your marriage has improved," Dr. Riley said.

"Thank you," Anna said then turned to Kulap. "You're a lucky woman."

"That I am," Kulap said as she interlaced her fingers with Dr. Riley's then continued, "sometimes being the second wife pays off. They've already had practice."

Dr. Riley laughed then turned to Anna. "It sounds like your husband's a lucky guy."

"I feel pretty fortunate too," Anna replied before they walked off. "Enjoy your first night in the house!"

~~~

Kulap relaxed in a black nightie on the floor of their new home on a cashmere blanket. Dr. Riley took in the sight of his wife.

The two had decided to spend the night "camping" in the living room of their new lake house. All of their furniture and belongings would arrive the next day, but for now it was just the two of them living out the perfect empty nest life, complete with champagne and a decadent dessert.

"I could get used to this," Kulap said as Dr. Riley gently held a fork full of chocolate cake to her lips. Kulap slowly chewed as Dr. Riley leaned back on his forearms and looked out the landscape window. The moon's light reflected off the dark waters of the lake that gently rolled in the breeze.

This truly was the life he imagined.

Chapter 2

Podcast #2
The Inevitable Collision of
Negative Relationship Patterns (NRPs)

"In this new model for relationships and marriage, we *build in* the expectation for the inevitable collision of NRPs. It will naturally occur in all relationships and we all have to expect this and be prepared for it. The term Negative Relationship Pattern (NRP) is defined here as any negative behavior that hurts the relationship and damages emotional closeness or loving feelings. No one is perfect. Everyone enters into a relationship with subtle, deeply ingrained Negative Relationship Patterns that inevitably collide and cause recurring conflict.

Unfortunately, couples are not prepared to encounter negative aspects of their partners' behavior. They react with hurt and resentment, which can build up over time and seriously affect emotional closeness and feelings of love."

Daniel and Heather Green were back in Dr. Riley's office for their second session. It had been a week since they'd last seen Dr. Riley and they had already discussed some of their communication problems after listening to that week's podcast. They had made a commitment to listen to his weekly podcasts and discuss them afterwards to further reinforce what they were

11

learning in between their weekly counseling sessions. They looked forward every week to learning new things to apply in their own relationship. Now that they were here with Dr. Riley again, they were ready to go further.

"Here's how we can dive a little deeper," Dr. Riley said as he handed Heather and Daniel each a piece of paper. "I want you to use this worksheet to explore your Negative Relationship Patterns and your Love Needs."

"Our what?" Daniel asked.

The Greens looked at the paper. On it was two sections. One was a breakdown of the twenty most common Negative Relationship Patterns and the second was a list of questions to ask to explore Love Needs.

Heather started to browse through the list of Negative Relationship Patterns, or NRPs. On the list were things that she recognized in her husband: *Has a problem with control of anger and temper. Interrupts me when I'm talking.* And things that she recognized in herself: *Overly passive, doesn't speak up with opinions and is passive aggressive: punishing me with emotional distance.*

Daniel read it over too and saw himself in various NRPs like: *Doesn't share enough or talk with me about the day and the things that happened.* And saw Heather in the: *Overly critical.*

As they continued to read the worksheet, Dr. Riley gave them further instructions. "Daniel, I need you to go through this list and mark off all the things that you think you do that are negative in the relationship. And Heather, you'll do the same. Then you'll both go back over the list and mark the NRPs your partner does that make you unhappy and cause problems in the relationship. Then find the top three NRPs you want the other to work on and talk it over. After that, you'll discuss your Love Needs."

Dr. Riley saw the wheels spin in each of their heads. He could feel their apprehension.

"There's no right or wrong here," he said. "Just simply ask each other what the other needs to feel deeply loved. Then you'll write it down in their words, not your loose translation of it. Then, if it feels vague, ask them what it looks like specifically."

"How are we supposed to do this?" Heather asked. Dr. Riley, always on his toes, was quick to reply.

"Earlier when we talked about communication you said, 'we don't talk', and Daniel replied that 'we talk.' Neither one of you was wrong, but Heather what did you really mean specifically?"

Heather paused for a second then replied, "I meant that we only talk about the mundane surface level stuff like the kids' schedules or the balance of our bank account. I don't know how he feels about work or the fact that his mother is sick right now. And because he's not sharing, I feel like it's inappropriate for me to share. Like we don't have that level of trust anymore."

Dr. Riley then turned to Daniel who looked shocked. "How do you feel in hearing what Heather just said?"

Daniel paused before responding, then softly replied, "I didn't know that's what she meant. I thought she wanted to nag me to talk because she was tired of talking to the kids all day."

Dr. Riley nodded his head in a gesture of understanding. "Do you see where the gap in communication lies here?"

"Yeah, obviously," Daniel replied.

"So, do you think you could commit to sharing a bit more about how you feel about the things that happen in your day to day?"

"Of course, that would help me too. I sometimes feel like I have to handle everything myself. I would love to unload some of this," Daniel said.

"And I would love to help you get through it," Heather replied as she reached over and squeezed Daniel's thigh in a gesture of solidarity.

Dr. Riley put down the pad of paper he'd been taking notes on. "See, you're already making progress. Do you think you can handle this assignment?"

Heather and Daniel nodded in agreement and Dr. Riley sent them on their way to work through their Negative Relationship Patterns and Love Needs.

~~~

"These NRPs are damaging to a relationship in two ways. First, these are negative behaviors that frustrate and turn off each partner, creating conflict. Second, these complaints also often reflect a failure to meet the deeper Love

Needs of a partner," Dr. Steve Riley's voice boomed over the speakers of the fifteen-foot U-Haul Truck driven by George Applebaum. George, short for Georgia, was speeding north along I-35 headed straight towards the Minneapolis area. She and her wife Nola, the epitome of the middle America girl next door, had spent the last four days trekking from Los Angeles to the great state of Minnesota.

"Wasn't the first podcast episode enough?" Nola asked as she turned down the volume.

"No. I want more of a sense of who he is," George replied.

"You're worried about figuring my dad out now? When we're forty-five minutes from his place?" Nola asked. George, a curly haired high-lighted brunette with a father who had rebelled against his Jewish upbringing, was nervous to meet her father-in-law for the first time.

"It's worth a shot," George shrugged and turned the volume back up on the podcast version of Dr. Steve Riley's "Relationship Co-Coaching." "Also, I think it's good for us to listen to his advice."

"True," Nola said. She knew her dad had a lot of great information to give, and the first episode had already begun to shape their own conversations about their relationship.

Ever since George and Nola had hit the road, they'd been discussing their Negative Relationship Patterns and Love Needs. In their conversations they'd arrived at the fact that George needed to feel valued to feel deeply loved and Nola needed a partner she could rely on. They had both agreed to work on providing these things for each other, but as it was in most relationships, they knew it would take work.

Nola and George had been together for just over a year and they were still figuring each other out. They had met on set and started dating secretly. Quickly, they became entrenched in each other's lives. Before they knew it, they were married with a little one on the way. Life was incredibly good for them until reality hit and they both realized that having a child required them to be a lot more responsible than they had been. This was part of the reason they were moving back to Minnesota.

At that moment, George looked over at Nola and placed a hand on Nola's protruding belly. George had never seen her wife so full of life.

"What if your dad hates me?" George asked.

"It's going to be fine," Nola said. "My dad's always been warm and welcoming to all my friends."

"Your friends? I'm a friend?" George sighed.

"You know what I mean," Nola said. "He's open. He's going to be excited for us."

"You didn't tell him yet, did you?"

"About us? Of course. He knows I have a girlfriend," Nola said.

"What about a wife?"

"I thought I'd surprise him. After all he didn't get to walk me down the aisle," Nola said with a smile.

"You're the one who wanted to elope." George removed her hand from Nola's belly and gripped the steering wheel.

"I know. I know. I'm kidding. I would've died if we had to do the whole pomp and circumstance of it all. You know that," Nola replied.

"Of course. But he's excited that you're moving home, right?"

Nola paused then turned to stare out the window.

"You didn't tell him that either?" George exclaimed. Nola's passivity was one of the Negative Relationship Patterns they had discussed on the drive east and yet she had never mentioned the fact that Dr. Riley had no clue they were moving in with him the entire ride.

"I told him. He just misinterpreted it and I didn't correct him."

"So, what? He thinks we drove across the country to come by and say hi?" George asked out of frustration. This was a pain point for her. It bugged her that Nola shied away from being assertive especially in situations like this.

"Sort of. Maybe. I told him we were taking a road trip and that we'd probably stop in."

"And by stop in you mean show up with a wife, a baby on the way, and a truck full of all our crap?" George said sternly. Nola's inability to face confrontation was another repeating pattern that often affected George's life. However, whenever George brought the Negative Relationship Pattern up, Nola tended to brush it off as if it was no big deal. "Everything always works out," Nola would say, stating that she didn't see the point of being confrontational. George on the other hand needed Nola to step up and talk to her father about them moving in. She wanted Dr. Riley to accept her into the family and since Nola didn't have her back it made her worry.

"This is so not the way I wanted to make my first impression," George said.

"If it makes you feel better, I'll get out of the truck first and tell him everything," Nola replied. She could tell George was frustrated and she really was trying to work on her own negative patterns.

"You will?" George asked.

"Of course. Everything's going to be fine. Besides, my dad loves surprises," Nola said then leaned over and kissed George on the cheek. "It keeps the relationship fresh."

~ ~ ~

"I didn't want any surprises," Dr. Riley said when Kulap asked him why he was home early from work.

"You didn't think I could handle the delivery guys alone?" Kulap asked.

"Of course, I did," Dr. Riley said. "But you know me, I get excited for new things." Though they had moved all of their other furniture into the lake home a week prior, today Dr. Riley's new furniture for his home office was being delivered.

Dr. Steve's office was technically in the basement, but since the house sat on a hill above the lake, the lower level acted as the first floor. The office was situated just below the living room and had an equally beautiful view out another giant picture window. Sliding glass doors on the left allowed access to the backyard and the dock below.

"It feels nice to be home, baby," Dr. Steve said as he wrapped his arms around his wife.

"It does," Kulap replied with a passionate kiss. "I could get used to you coming home early," Kulap said as she pulled away for a breath. Dr. Steve smiled and was about to go in for another kiss when a delivery guy knocked on the window. Dr. Steve and Kulap were startled at the sound and quickly stepped away from each other.

"Is this where you want the furniture?" the delivery guy asked. Dr. Steve nodded. "Great," the delivery guy said. "And hey, we're happy to help unload that other truck if you want. My guys could use the extra cash."

"What other truck?" Kulap asked with a surprised look on her face. She turned to her husband who simply shrugged his shoulders. He didn't know either.

~~~

Dr. Steve and Kulap quickly ran upstairs and emerged from the house to find a large UHaul with a worn-down Jeep attached to its hitch backing down their driveway.

"What in the--?" Kulap exclaimed. "I thought we just had one truck of furniture being dropped off."

"We did," Dr. Steve replied.

"So, what is this?" Kulap asked as she followed Dr. Steve towards the truck. Dr. Steve was about ten steps ahead of her, but still she could see a smile creeping across his face. Kulap softened as she caught up to him. She placed her hand on his shoulder. "Did you buy me that Peloton bike?"

Kulap had been wanting the at home spin bike for months but hadn't been able to justify the cost. However, she had been dropping hints to her husband in the hopes that maybe he'd buy her a small token of appreciation for fixing up their condo and helping the sale along so they could move into this house.

Dr. Steve shook his head no then kept walking. Kulap fell back a few steps as Dr. Steve started waving at whoever was emerging from the truck's passenger side.

"Nola!" Dr. Steve exclaimed. The UHaul came to a complete stop and so did Dr. Steve and Kulap. Slowly, Nola Riley made her way down from the bench seat of the truck. Dr. Steve paused for a moment at the sight of her, then lunged forward and grabbed Nola in a giant hug. "I can't believe you're here. And…"

"You're pregnant?!" Kulap said with a shock.

"Six and a half months," Nola beamed as she gently rubbed her belly in a mothering gesture. "Surprise!" she said.

Dr. Steve took a step back to look at her when it dawned on him. "I'm going to be a grandpa! Kulap, look at her."

"Oh, I'm looking." Kulap shook her head in disappointment. She was confused. She didn't expect to see Nola, especially not a pregnant Nola. "What are you doing here?"

"Remember, I told you she was on a road trip with her girlfriend and they might stop by. Didn't know it was today. But that's okay, this is a great surprise."

Kulap glared at the truck which was now moving further down the driveway. "This doesn't look like a stopover," she said.

"I'm sure there's an explanation," Dr. Steve replied as he put his arm around his only daughter.

"Of course, dad. Remember when we talked, and I said we were heading east? Well, the we isn't just my girlfriend. I'm married!" Nola said as she held up her left hand and flashed a modest band with a few tiny diamonds on it.

"Holy—" Kula started.

"It's pretty isn't it?" Nola sighed.

"No, no. I'm not talking about the ring. I'm talking about that." Kulap gestured towards the UHaul. Just then, a huge crack could be heard across the lawn.

"Was that our cherry tree?" Dr. Steve asked.

Kulap nodded then turned to Nola. "Who's driving that thing? Please tell me that's not your husband."

"You know she's a lesbian," Dr. Steve said.

"Yes. But she's also pregnant so forgive me if I made a quick assumption amidst the chaos."

"That's my wife, George. She drove the whole way. I couldn't with this and all," Nola said as she pointed to her bump.

"I can't believe you're married," Dr. Steve said.

"You're not mad you didn't get to walk me down the aisle, are you?" Nola asked.

"Of course not. I kind of figured one day you would just do it," Dr. Steve replied.

"I knew you'd understand," Nola said as she twisted her wedding ring around her finger in one smooth loop.

"He understands. But what he doesn't understand is that truck," Kulap added as she glared at the half toppled cherry tree.

"About that," Nola began. She was about to explain their whole story. How they had run out of money and needed a place to live. How they had attempted to rent a place in LA but had continuously run into problems. George's credit was terrible. Nola was out of work and the only place they could find was a studio in the worst part of town. They had both decided that a dump was no place to birth a child and figured they would head to Minnesota, get back on their feet, save some money, have the baby, then head back to Los Angeles and return to furthering their careers in the TV and film industry. But before Nola could say any more George came traipsing down the side of the driveway.

"Whoa. You guys are not going to believe this, but I totally did not see that coming," George said as she approached the group. "I'll fix it, dad. I promise." Without missing a beat George gave Dr. Steve a big hug hello. "Marrying your daughter has changed my life, sir."

"And I'm sure it's going to change ours too," Kulap added.

"Aren't you sweet?" George replied as she gave Kulap a smothering hug. Kulap managed to escape George's grip just as George turned to Nola. "So, they're cool with us moving in?"

Nola's eyes went wide. George stammered, trying to think of something to say.

Dr. Steve felt the tension rise in the air and did what he always did as the head of the household. "It's no big deal," he said. "Of course, you guys can live here. You know you've always been welcome to come home."

Kulap shook her head. She couldn't believe what Dr. Steve was saying. Clearly this was not something they had ever discussed when they made plans to purchase the home on Humble Lake.

"This is great, actually," Dr. Steve went on. "Your brother and Pilar are moving back to town next week. They might even stay a few days before they move into campus housing at Macalaster."

"They might?" Kulap asked with a deeply inquisitive look.

"Yeah. You knew that," Dr. Steve said.

"I guess I missed that one too," Kulap said. Clearly there was a lot she and her husband had neglected to discuss. "But don't worry, it's fine. It'll be perfectly nice to have the whole family together. Right, Nola?"

Nola smiled. Though Nola and Kulap always appeared to get along, there was an underlying tension between them. She'd never said it aloud but Nola felt Kulap had moved in far too soon after her mom passed and Kulap felt Nola had never welcomed her. George knew this, but George also knew that Nola would never say anything. She was far too passive.

~~~

While George and Nola unpacked their truck with the help of the delivery guys who Dr. Steve paid, Dr. Steve headed down to his office to arrange his new furniture. As he worked to set up his new space, Dr. Steve thought about his work with the Greens and his other clients. He thought about how Negative Relationship Patterns consistently showed up in every relationship and how if they weren't addressed tension would arise. He could tell by the way George had blurted out that they were moving in with him and Kulap that there were things she and Nola needed to work on.

"That's a beautiful view, Dad," a voice said interrupting Dr. Steve's train of thought. Nola stood in the doorway watching Dr. Steve set up his brand-new desk.

"Nola. Come in," Dr. Steve said as he motioned to the leather club chair in front of his desk. "It's good to have you here."

"Are you sure Kulap's okay with us moving in?" Nola asked as she took a seat.

Dr. Steve looked up from the desk. "It might take her a moment to get adjusted but it's fine," he said. "Is everything okay with you?

"Yeah," Nola said as she propped her legs up on the coffee table. Being pregnant made standing on her feet for long periods uncomfortable.

"That doesn't sound convincing," Dr. Steve said.

Nola took a deep breath then began, "I'm just worried about our future. I love George, but she's not exactly the most reliable and that really makes me feel uneasy. You know, we wouldn't be here unless we were totally desperate, and George hadn't completely maxed out all four of her credit cards converting an unused sound stage into a hydroponic pot farm."

Dr. Riley paused. He thought about going into a whole speech about how Negative Relationship Patterns are fallback behaviors popping up to the surface when communication goes badly thus fueling conflict, but when he saw how frustrated Nola appeared, he decided to give a simple piece of advice instead. "That sounds like an issue you need to discuss with your wife," Dr. Steve said as he put the pillowcases on the pillows.

"Wait. I thought you would've gotten all therapist on me. I'm your daughter. You're supposed to help me," Nola responded. Dr. Steve was about to reply when…

"What about me?" George's voice chimed in. Nola and Dr. Steve turned to the door and looked at her with shocked faces. It was clear George had been standing at the doorway for a few minutes and had heard everything.

Nola didn't care. "What about you? You got us into this mess. Let's get real here for just one second."

"First of all, you had a choice. We could've stayed in LA," George said defensively.

"And lived in that rat farm of a studio?" Nola gasped.

"Okay, fine. Maybe not. But I don't see how this is a mess. You're here with your family. In this gorgeous house," George said as she pointed at the lake just outside the window.

"She has a point," Dr. Steve said. "And you two are welcome to stay as long as you need."

"You see that, Nola? Problem solved. Now that's real love. Give me a high five, dad?" George held up her right palm and Dr. Steve gave her some skin.

The sight of this only made Nola madder. George only high-fived people for one reason. "O.m.g… you just smoked, didn't you?"

George sheepishly looked down at the ground. "…maybe?"

With that Nola stormed off, leaving Dr. Steve and George alone. Dr. Steve was about to follow Nola when George stopped him.

"For what it's worth sir, I appreciate you becoming so sensitive to my situation so fast. And for, you know, not judging me too harshly."

Dr. Steve paused and gestured for George to have a seat at his desk then took a seat on the chair opposite her. He could see George needed some direction and Dr. Riley was never one to pass up an opportunity to help a couple in need. "You two are in this together, George. Both of you have

NRPs you're bringing to the table and you're going to need to work on them as a couple."

"NRPs?" George asked.

"Negative Relationship Patterns. For instance, your bad decisions hurting career—"

"Oh, right! From your book," George exclaimed. She remembered the term immediately. George was never one for acronyms, she liked when things were fully spelled out for her.

"You read it?" Dr. Steve asked. He was surprised she had taken the time to read his book, but also proud to know it had reached all the way to Los Angeles. Albeit, she was married to his daughter so that might have been the reason she had a copy. Still, Dr. Steve always loved to hear from his readers.

"Are you kidding me? I read it cover to cover. Admittedly, I was pretty zooted, sir, when I read it. So, I'm a little foggy on the details. But I get what you mean about all the NPRs."

"NRPs," Dr. Steve corrected her.

"Right," George replied. "So, now what? I go and talk to Nola?"

"That would be a good start," Dr. Steve said. The room got silent for a moment.

"Oh, you mean like now?" George realized.

Dr. Steve nodded.

"I was just hoping we'd get a little more time together. You could give me some more advice?" George pleaded.

"We'll have plenty of time to talk. Go find Nola," Dr. Steve replied.

"Okay, dad. See you later then." With that George rose from her seat and walked towards the office door.

~~~

George found Nola in the guest bedroom unpacking her suitcase. Nola ignored her when she entered the room.

"Don't do that," George said. "I know this is hard for you, but you can't go into your shell like you always do."

"I was trying to talk to him," Nola said with a sigh.

"And I heard that. But I also heard you blaming me for us having to move. We're in this together you know," George replied. "You can't keep ignoring your problems and hope they'll work out. You have to talk to me." It really aggravated George that Nola would go to her dad with her frustrations about their money issues but not talk to her. Nola had never brought it up before, just simply suggested they move to Minnesota to save money then gone along with whatever George planned after that.

"I'm sorry I should've come to you instead of him. But you also know that I need you to be a little more reliable," Nola said turning the tables and pointing out one of George's Negative Relationship Patterns.

"And I'm trying. We're here aren't we? This is our time to start over and get back on our feet," George said then remembered one of the things Nola had told her in the car about how she needed financial security to feel safe in the relationship. "Would it make you feel better if I told you that I was already looking for a job?" Nola finally looked up from unpacking her suitcase.

"It's not illegal is it?" Nola asked.

"Why would you ask that?"

"George, we just left LA because you grew marijuana in a soundstage you had no permission to use," Nola said.

"You have a point. Okay, I promise to find a legit, grown-up job," George said as she lovingly looked Nola in the eyes. She then took the palm of Nola's hand in her own and said "Seriously, I want you to know that you can depend on me and you don't have to worry."

This felt like a soothing balm for Nola, quieting at least for a moment her fears about whether life would be safe for her in the future with George. A deep feeling of love and affection flooded her. So, when George said, "But you need to work on your stuff too." Nola smiled coyly and replied. "Fine. I promise to be more assertive." Then grabbed George by the hand, snuggled up next to her and said, "Let's sit for just a few minutes, relax, and take in the view of the lake before unpacking everything."

Chapter 3

Podcast #3
Relationship Problems Caused by Failure to Fulfill Unique Love Needs

---

"It has become overwhelmingly evident to me after years of practicing marriage therapy that there's one fundamental cause for all relationship problems: the unique *Love Needs* of one or both partners are not being met after repeated efforts to communicate these needs. Subsequently, deep-rooted feelings of frustration turn to chronic resentment and anger, which then result in emotional distance.

This is simple and intuitive. In this case the term *Love Need* is defined as a core need to feel deeply loved in a way unique to you and your personal preferences, ideals, and values in life. If your partner does not meet these love needs, unhappiness is inevitable.

The solution would seem to be so incredibly clear, why don't we make the purpose of romantic relationships and marriage to be the mutual fulfillment of love needs? Doesn't everyone deserve to be loved in the ways that they need to feel truly happy?"

Heather and Daniel Green had returned to Dr. Riley's for their third session. Though they were optimistic about the process as it had gone so far, they both were feeling a bit nervous about the homework they had been given.

Their assignment had been to discuss their Negative Relationship Patterns and Love Needs, but their discussion had ended in a standstill. Even though they'd listened to episode three of the podcast, they were still struggling.

"We really tried to talk through our Love Needs, but it kind of felt like we were going in circles. I kept telling him that I wanted to feel appreciated, and he kept saying that he appreciated me and that's why he always bought me nice gifts."

"What's so wrong with that?" Daniel asked.

"I love everything you've ever given me, but that doesn't make me feel loved," Heather replied then turned to Dr. Riley to explain. "I guess I'm more of an acts of service kind of person," Heather said in reference to the book *The Five Love Languages* written by Dr. Gary Chapman. It helps readers discover their primary "love language" through self-assessment based upon a general classification of five need areas—words of affirmation, receiving gifts, quality time, acts of service, and physical touch.

Dr. Riley was familiar with the book, but in his experience with Relationship Co-Coaching there was far more to Love Needs than a simple self-assessment based upon just five broad based categories. Though he saw the importance of understanding the love languages as described by Dr. Chapman, he believed that even when couples were helped to understand their partner's Love Needs, they still often failed to fulfill them.

"I think I see how you two got stuck," Dr. Riley said. "First, let me explain something. When I talk about Love Needs, I'm not talking about the five love languages as you might know them. I'm talking about what you truly need to feel loved. Acts of service might be your love language, Heather, but what does that mean to you? What would that need look like if it were being met?" Dr. Riley asked.

Heather thought about this for a moment. She'd never been asked to be specific, but there was plenty she wanted out of her relationship. "I'd like Daniel to do nice things for me," she said.

"I do nice things. I did all the dishes last night," Daniel said.

"After I asked you to," Heather replied.

"Okay, but that was still a nice thing he did, right?" Dr. Riley asked.

"Sure. But that doesn't make me feel loved when I have to ask for it," Heather explained.

"Okay. So, what would make you feel loved? What can Daniel do to show you he appreciates you?" Dr. Riley prodded.

Heather thought for another moment then realized what she wanted was Daniel to pick up the slack without her having to ask him. She wanted to feel like he had her back, like they were a team. "You know what would be nice," Heather began. "Is if on the days that Daniel gets home early, he took charge and figured out dinner for us instead of waiting for me to come home exhausted from work and relying on me to do everything."

"How does that sound Daniel?" Dr. Riley asked.

"Simple. I can do that," Daniel replied.

"Great. So, Heather, do you see how simply giving a concrete example to Daniel helps him understand what you need?"

Heather nodded.

"And, Daniel, do you see how by asking a few more questions I was able to help Heather reveal what she really meant when she said she wanted to feel appreciated?"

"Absolutely," Daniel replied. "When you explain it the way you did, it all seems so easy."

"It's easy once you understand that it takes a while to understand what we really need ourselves. However, once we can drill this down by asking the following questions: What would this need look like if it were being met? How does my partner not meet this need right now? In what way are they meeting this need already? We can create an understanding of what each other truly needs to feel loved. Do you think you two could do the assignment now?"

Daniel and Heather both looked at each other, smiled then nodded yes.

"I'm really glad we came back," Heather said.

"We were always coming back," Daniel said then turned to Dr. Riley. "Though, if you'd seen the way we were arguing over our Love Needs assignment you might not have wanted us back," Daniel laughed.

"Of course, I would. So, see you next week?" Dr. Riley asked.

"Absolutely," Heather replied.

~~~

After his session, Dr. Riley headed directly home. Normally, he would meet with his producer, Ryan, and discuss upcoming podcast episodes, but today his son Kevin and his wife, Pilar would be arriving, and he wanted to be there when they got to the house.

At the Minneapolis-St. Paul International airport, Kevin, who was a younger spitting image of his father, and Pilar Riley piled their luggage on top of a rent-a-cart. Pilar, a strong Afro-Latina whose parents had met in NYC in grad school, had her headphones on and was listening to Dr. Riley's podcast. "One of the chief contributing factors as to why partners fail to meet each other's Love Needs is repeating conflict. Are there any 'communication issues' in your relationship? Is there conflict or unspoken tension you want to reduce for a more relaxed, loving relationship? If you're like most couples, your answer to both questions will likely be *yes*," Dr. Riley's voice said. Pilar nodded in agreement as if Dr. Riley were standing right there before her.

"What are you listening to?" Kevin asked.

"Relationship Co-Coaching," Pilar said in a matter of fact manner. She had listened to every episode so far. So had Kevin, though he did it a little more out of obligation than a sense of wanting to learn. He knew all about his dad's teachings. He had grown up with him after all and had heard his dad talking to his mom about Love Needs and NRPs and the like. When the podcast came out, Pilar, whose mother had worked as a social worker in her native Colombia when she was younger, had become fascinated with his dad's work and asked Kevin to participate more in their relationship in a co-coaching sort of way. Kevin had agreed and they were currently working on understanding each other's Love Needs. However, they were also currently standing in a busy airport.

"Can you turn that off for a minute?" Kevin asked.

"Sure," Pilar said as she took the earbuds out of her ears and placed them in her purse.

"I just want to say that when we get there, you should probably let me do the talking," Kevin said as they walked outside and down an outdoor corridor.

"And *why* would I do that exactly?" Pilar asked.

"Because I haven't exactly asked my dad if we can stay there?" Kevin said sheepishly.

When Pilar had been accepted into Macalester University's PhD program in International Relations, she had hesitated. While she loved Kevin's family, and found his father to be a kind, generous and smart man, she worried that living so close to him would send Kevin into a type of regressive behavior where he would act like a young son again. She worried he wouldn't be the husband and man she saw deep within him. This was something they had discussed at length. One of her Love Needs was that she needed Kevin to be as equally strong as her and being strong meant that he took charge when she needed him to. Kevin had assured Pilar that he would handle their living situation. Since she would be giving up her job at a thinktank in D.C. and her full scholarship stipend would be minimal, and Macalester's program was one of the best in the nation, Pilar cast her fears aside and agreed with Kevin's suggestion that they live at his dad's place to save money for a future home. Of course, all of that was predicated on Kevin taking charge and fulfilling her need of a man who she could count on.

"I can't believe you didn't talk to your dad like you promised," she said. "You know I don't like it when you say things and don't follow through." This was one of Pilar's other Love Needs that she'd made clear to Kevin before they even thought of moving.

"Trust me. I know how to handle my dad," Kevin replied as his phone buzzed with an alert. "That's our car." He nodded in the direction of a silver Prius. Kevin waved to the driver as he pushed the cart to an open space on the curb. Pilar followed close behind, pondering the fact that Kevin hadn't followed through.

"Give me your phone," Pilar said as she snatched it out of his hands.

"Hey," Kevin said. "What are you doing?"

"I'm calling Dr. Steve," Pilar said as she pushed a few buttons.

"Why do you always call him that? Why can't you call him dad? Or simply Steve?"

"You want to know why Kevin? It's about respect. You better believe that when I finish my PhD program everyone will be calling me doctor."

"Okay," Kevin said as he waved at their car. "I don't want to argue. I get it."

"We're not arguing. I'm simply calling your dad to tell him we're moving in."

Kevin turned to her. "Please don't. I promise this will all work out. Remember how I promised you that we'd get married and move to D.C. and we'd live in that apartment you wanted that had ten people bidding on it and I got it?" When he put his mind to it, Kevin was good at following through.

"Fine." Pilar handed Kevin's phone back to him and helped the driver with the luggage. "I'll get those," she said to him.

"Why don't you let him help?" Kevin said.

"Because that's how it starts, Kevin, behind a shield of chivalry." Pilar turned to the driver and continued, "Don't worry, it won't affect your tip. I respect you as a disenfranchised wage earner, regardless of your gender."

The driver looked at her with a puzzled look.

"Please excuse my wife, it's been a long day of traveling. She hasn't been able to be in control of anything for going on five hours now."

"You make an excellent point," Pilar said with a surprising smile. Normally, she would've had a conversation with Kevin to discuss how his NRP—passive aggressiveness—affected her, but she had a better idea.

"Driver, may I call you Bill?"

"Sure, why not?" the driver shrugged.

"If I agree to give you an extra ten percent tip would you let me drive?"

"I mean. I don't know, m'am. I feel like we'd be entering into a whole new world of legality here if I let you do that."

"I'm not interested in antiquated approaches to inferior business practices," Pilar said as she placed her hands on her hips. "This is your car, right? You didn't sign away any rights to it did you?"

"No," Bill replied.

"And you're just a contract employee, correct?" Pilar asked.

"I suppose that's correct," Bill replied.

"So, technically, if I drove this Prius of yours, I'd just be driving a friend's car."

"Are we friends?" Bill asked, missing the point.

"How long have you been driving today, Bill?" Pilar asked taking a different tack.

Bill looked at his watch. "I've been at it since six this morning. That's when my local doughnut shop opens."

Pilar looked at her watch. "And it's now three o'clock."

"What time were you going to work 'til?'"

"I don't know, seven, eight tonight."

"That's well over twelve hours Bill. That's unsafe. Truck drivers can't even drive for over eleven hours a day. Does driving this car seem safe, Bill?"

Bill shook his head. "I guess I could use a break."

"That's exactly what I was trying to say, Bill. So, I can drive?" Pilar asked.

Bill tried to think of a good reason to say no, but he had no argument to match Pilar's. Pilar knew this and held out her hand. Bill relented and gently placed his keys in her hand. Pilar smiled and headed straight to the driver's side.

As Pilar opened the driver's side door, Kevin made a move to get into the passenger's seat, but Pilar stopped him. "You get in the back," she said. "This is Bill's car. He gets to ride up front."

Without another word, Kevin slid into the backseat as Bill fastened himself into the front seat. Pilar adjusted the rearview mirror and honed on Kevin. "What's the address again?"

"Ninety-five Larch," Kevin said without looking at her. He was fixated on a couple outside the window with a small kid. The mother sat patiently waiting as her husband took charge and loaded the luggage into a taxi. The father then continued to help the mom and child get situated before he took a seat shotgun. Kevin sighed at the sight. He wished he could take control more often. He knew Pilar wanted him to be more reliable, but she also made it difficult for him. This was one of the dilemmas they faced when trying to fulfill each other's Love Needs.

"You got that, Bill?" Pilar asked.

"Ay, ay, Captain," Bill replied as he entered the address into his phone. Pilar peeled out of the airport as Bill began navigating.

As they drove, Kevin took note of the familiar setting. When the Riley family had gone on vacations as kids, Kevin's mom would always point out the beauty of Minnesota every time they returned. She and Dr. Steve loved showing their kids the world, but she never wanted them to forget where they came from. Kevin and Pilar had lived in D.C. for two years now and had yet to fly back home. They spent most holidays with her family and on two occasions Dr. Steve and Kulap had come to Washington D.C.—once in the winter to see the White House lit up for Christmas, and once in the spring to view the cherry blossoms.

Kevin thought about the life they were leaving behind in the city. He had been working at an upscale restaurant in the congressional district waiting tables and learning the ins and outs of the industry. He had planned to work there for another year until he would embark on his own project—a master puppetry dinner theatre, but when Pilar got it in her head that she wanted to go back to school there was no stopping her. Besides, Kevin could never ask Pilar to put aside her dreams. He deeply understood that one of her Love Needs was him supporting her in becoming successful. She was on a mission to become the first Afro-latina American to succeed in politics. Her heritage and proving that she had everything it took to compete in a white world was a major part of who she was. When they'd discussed the move, Kevin insisted they go. His dreams could always wait, Macalester and the full ride couldn't.

"Bill, tell me about this job of yours. Is this your future?" Pilar asked.

"I mean, it's my present, so I guess it's the future for now," Bill replied.

"Oh, Bill. We have a lot to talk about," Pilar said. As Pilar continued to talk to Bill about his future, Kevin continued to look out the window and reminisce.

They drove past a sign for the Mall of America, and Kevin remembered his ninth birthday party. It was held at the mini-amusement park in the middle of the mall and his mom had made her famous berry cake and decorated it to look like a roller coaster. That was one of his best birthdays ever, well, besides the time Pilar had gotten them into the Smithsonian after hours to view the Puppets on Radio, Film, and Television exhibit. Pilar had a friend at the museum who had granted them exclusive access plus a behind the scenes tour where Kevin was allowed to puppeteer one of the original Muppets. That was one of the greatest moments of Kevin's life, it was also why he loved Pilar so much. To others she might seem controlling, but to Kevin, Pilar was an amazingly strong woman who knew how to make the impossible happen. Kevin admired that in her. He looked longingly at her through the rearview mirror as he snapped out of his train of thought and honed on the conversation she was having with Bill.

"You don't drive the car, Bill. The car drives you," Pilar said. Kevin smiled. He loved the way his wife exuded confidence when she talked about social injustices.

"No, I think that would be one of those self-driving deals, like a Tesla or something," Bill replied.

"I'm speaking metaphorically, Bill. Let me put it another way, if I crash this car and you wind up flying through the windshield, is employer-provided insurance going to pay a cosmetic surgeon to fix your face?"

Bill was crestfallen. She had a point. "I can't even get my crappy HMO to reimburse me for my calf augmentation." he said.

"That kind of sounds like elective surgery, Bill," Kevin chimed in with a laugh.

"Elective? There's nothing elective about these!" Bill kicked a leg up onto the dashboard. "See!"

Kevin locked eyes with Pilar in the rearview mirror. "Turn right up there."

Pilar made a sharp turn up the private road. "You can put your gams away, Bill," Pilar said as the Riley driveway came into full view. Though she appreciated Bill's comic relief she needed to prepare for what was to come.

Entering the Riley house, especially when she knew she and Kevin weren't being fully honest with their intentions, always brought on some anxiety. Pilar wasn't sure if it was the stigma of in-laws, or just the fact that she always felt like she had to prove herself to Kulap. She had loved Kevin's mom and was devastated when she passed. When Kulap entered their lives, she had tried to be welcoming but Kulap always seemed to keep them at an arm's distance.

Once Pilar parked the car, Bill hopped out and went straight to the trunk. Pilar started marching after him. "Bill, you know that's my—"

"Pilar, don't even start," Bill shouted. "You gave me a little break from driving. Let me help here."

Pilar relented and backed off to allow Bill to pull the luggage out of the trunk.

"I hope you'll think about our talk, Bill. And really advocate for yourself. If there's one thing we all have, it's our voices," Pilar said. "Kevin, make sure you give Bill a bigger tip."

Without a word Kevin pulled out his phone and proceeded to add more money to Bill's tip on the rideshare app.

Pilar gave Bill a firm handshake to thank him for the "ride" then sent him on his way.

Once Bill's car had disappeared down the driveway, Pilar turned to Kevin to discuss the situation at hand. "I feel weird about this," Pilar said. She didn't like holding secrets especially from Dr. Steve who was always so focused on creating lines of open and honest communication.

"Pilar, it's fine. I'm not about to overwhelm the man. He and Kulap just moved in here a week ago and Nola and George showed up a few days later with a moving van," Kevin said as he picked up their bags and headed to the front door.

"What? I didn't know that," Pilar said following him.

"My dad just told me this morning. And, if there's anything I know about him, it's that he only likes one big change at a time. Remember when we were planning the wedding and Nola told Dad that she was moving to London?"

"That was an April Fool's joke," Pilar replied.

"And yet he still freaked out," Kevin said. "Just trust me."

"I don't know," Pilar started. "Maybe we should've just moved into the dorms."

"And pose as paupers when we can live like kings? Where's the fun in that?" Kevin replied as they arrived at the precipice of the Riley home. Before Pilar could respond they were interrupted by a voice.

"Champagne?" They turned towards the front door to find a man standing in the open foyer with a bottle of bubbly and two glasses.

"Chet?" Kevin asked surprised to find one of his dad's old buddies answering the door.

"That's me!," Chet, the perennial bachelor, exclaimed. He took in the sight of Kevin then continued on, "Kevin, you're all grown up, man. I haven't seen you in years."

"Are you the welcoming crew?" Pilar asked. Chet was dressed in a vintage Hawaiian shirt and khaki cargo shorts. His blonde hair was a messy tuft atop his head.

"Nah, Chet's an old friend of my dad's. He's always around. Right, Chet?" Kevin said.

"Something like that. I came to toast your dad's new house but he's flitting around here like a little butterfly. Left me here to drink alone. Your sister and her wife are out. Kulap's somewhere. You sure you guys don't want to join?" Chet asked.

Pilar took one look at Kevin and their suitcases and another look at the champagne and made a quick decision. "Actually, I'll join you," she said. "Kevin has to go talk to his dad anyway."

~~~

Kevin found his dad downstairs in the office. Dr. Steve looked up from his computer. "Kevin," he said then made his way over to hug his son. "It's good to see you."

"You too, dad," Kevin said as he pulled away from the embrace.

"Did you see your sister, yet?" Dr. Steve asked.

"Not yet. We just walked in and I heard she's out with George. Pilar's upstairs drinking champagne with Chet."

"He's still here?" Dr. Steve asked as he shook his head.

"Seems so," Kevin replied.

"I was just finishing up some work so I could move my computer upstairs. It's been nice having a little space down here away from the chaos up there. I love having your sister and George here, but Kulap and I are not used to having others around," Dr. Steve said.

"I bet," Kevin said as he shifted his weight from foot to foot.

"You and Pilar can have this room. How many days are you staying again?"

"Just a few," Kevin replied without a second thought. This was definitely not the right time to tell his dad that he and Pilar were planning on moving in too.

"Great. I'll have Kulap bring down some towels and I'll help you set up the air mattress later. There's a bathroom just down the hall. It's meant to be for anyone who comes off the lake so it's a little tiny, but it should do."

"It's perfect, dad," Kevin replied.

"I'm glad you're back. It'll be nice having you around," Dr. Steve said.

"I'm glad to be home." Kevin watched as his dad walked off and thought about the fact that maybe things were a little bit more complicated than he thought and it wasn't going to be so easy to talk to his dad about moving in.

~~~

Upstairs in the kitchen, Pilar and Chet were two glasses deep into the bottle of champagne. Through their tipsiness they had become fast friends.

"I like you Chet. You say it how it is," Pilar said as she held up her glass to cheers him. "To new friends!" Chet said.

"Salud!" Pilar replied as she toasted him. They both drained the remaining half of their glasses in a single gulp. Pilar poured more champagne into the glasses then said, "What else should we drink to?"

"To being single," Chet said. Just then Dr. Steve entered.

"Woah. Slow down there," Dr. Steve said as he put out his hand and stopped Chet from bringing the glass to his lips. "Did something happen with Bree?"

Chet put the glass down and got a little teary eyed. "It's over, buddy. It's all over."

Chet went on to explain to Pilar and Dr. Steve that he had come home the night before at four thirty-five in the morning and Bree had been incredibly upset.

"Were you cheating?" Pilar asked.

"No of course not," Chet replied. "They'd made me Dungeon Master at my dungeons and dragons club. It's a tremendous responsibility."

"Is it Chet?" Dr. Steve asked in a serious tone.

"Yes. Lives, future fates and fortunes, they all rested in my hands." Chet said in a dead serious tone.

"I thought we'd talked about this," Dr. Steve said.

"Are you going to talk about Love Needs again? Because I gave Bree attention. We had an intense make-out session right before I went out. But that didn't stop her from packing up all her stuff and leaving."

"I'm pretty sure we discussed the fact that Bree's Love Need of attention was more than just physical," Dr. Steve said.

"I know," Chet said, hanging his head low.

"Sorry about that Chet," Pilar said. Chet nodded thanks as Pilar turned to Dr. Riley, "Did you talk to Kevin?"

"Yep. He's downstairs in my office unpacking your suitcases."

Pilar was surprised to hear this news. "So, you guys really did talk?"

"Yeah, of course why wouldn't we? It's gonna be a great couple of days having you here. And then once you move into campus housing it'll be nice to have you just down the street."

"It sure will be," Pilar said as she downed the rest of her glass. "Mind if I have the rest?" Pilar asked Chet as she picked up the bottle of champagne and walked off.

~~~

Pilar took the champagne straight downstairs where she found Kevin unpacking.

"Looks like you're having fun," Kevin said at the sight of Pilar and the alcohol.

"I'd be having a better time if your dad hadn't just told me he was looking forward to the next couple days of us staying here," Pilar said.

"I couldn't tell him. The timing was bad," Kevin said.

"That sounds like an excuse," Pilar replied. "We talked about this. I thought I made it clear that I needed you to take charge. That that would make me feel better about us living here. Otherwise, Kevin, I would've figured out the campus housing thing myself."

"I know. But you have to understand that the situation is a little more complicated. I couldn't tell him after he had just told me how chaotic things have been with Nola and George living here."

"This is what I was afraid of," Pilar sighed. "That you would resort back to being an insecure young boy again, scared to talk to your father."

"I'm not scared of him. I just want it to be right," Kevin said.

"Do you think the right time could be tomorrow?" Pilar asked with a serious face.

"Yes," Kevin replied. He knew that look and he knew that Pilar needed reassurance. "I promise. I want things to be good between us."

"Me too," Pilar said then softened. She and Kevin had worked through much bigger problems in the past. She knew he would talk to his father as promised. "I trust you."

"And I've got your back," Kevin said as he pulled Pilar into an embrace. Pilar melted in his arms. She loved Kevin. Though she often became frustrated with the fact that he didn't always follow through, she liked that he didn't take everything in life so seriously.

Aware that she had been pushing him to better meet her love needs she made a conscious attempt in that moment to fulfill one of his: "You know, I was thinking. As much as I don't want you to resort back to acting like a kid again, I do think us living here will be good for your creativity."

"Really?" Kevin asked. Though Pilar had been supportive of his ideas, she hadn't always been encouraging. So hearing this really affected Kevin and made him feel loved.

"Yeah," Pilar replied. "What's more inspiring for puppets than old childhood haunts?"

"It was here that I had originally thought of the idea," Kevin said.

"See, I think we're going to be just fine," Pilar said.

"Me too," Kevin replied then flopped himself onto the bed and gestured for her to join him. She placed her head on his chest and draped her arm over him. Together they lay in silence soaking in the moment, a moment that made them both feel really loved. Kevin felt supported in his pursuit of an unconventional career and Pilar felt satisfied that he had promised to talk with his father the next day. They had touched one another's Love Needs which drew them closer. After a few minutes passed, Kevin kissed the top of Pilar's head then asked, "So, are you going to share that bottle with me now?"

They sat up in bed and Pilar handed over her glass of champagne then raised the bottle up to cheers him. "To new starts," she said.

"To pursuing our dreams," Kevin added. They looked each other in the eyes, then took a sip of their drinks and enjoyed the intimacy of being in the moment together.

Part 2:
Now the Serious Relationship
Work Really Begins

Chapter 4

Podcast #4
Lack of Specificity in Love Needs!

"Although the idea of Love Needs is not new, couples often fail to meet Love Needs. Why? Much of the problem is that the reasons for doing so have not been more fully addressed. The first root cause is lack of clear definition of Love Needs. Because there is so little emphasis placed upon the idea of meeting Love Needs in our society, it's very common for couples to have difficulty identifying and articulating them.

Usually they are communicated in the form of generalizations, such as not showing enough appreciation, being disrespectful, needing quality time, helping out around the house, etc. The problem is that each of these words will most likely mean entirely different things to different people, so you must communicate with far greater specificity!"

Yesterday, the Greens had listened to episode four of Dr. Riley's podcast about specificity in Love Needs. Today, they were back in his office working on their relationship. They had been discussing each other's Love Needs but had hit a bump in the road.

Heather had told Daniel that she needed him to listen to her more and Daniel had countered that he always listened to Heather's problems. While this was true in some form, Heather still felt her need was not being met. It had become clear to them and to Dr. Riley that the lack of specificity around the concept of listening had led to their disagreement.

"Why don't you tell him what you really mean when you say he doesn't listen? Because, I would argue that Daniel is listening it's just not in the way you want," Dr. Riley said.

"You're right," Heather said then turned to Daniel. "I know you listen. But I also know that when I'm talking, I can see the wheels turning in your head the whole time. You're already coming up with a solution and all the things you want to say instead of really listening to what I'm saying."

"Do you hear what she's stating, Daniel?" Dr. Riley asked.

"I guess. But what am I supposed to do? Say nothing?" Daniel sighed.

"Of course not. Heather, what would you like Daniel to do?" Dr. Riley asked. "Be specific."

"I'd like him to really listen. To not be jumping ahead and zoning out to come up with an answer. I want to feel heard," Heather replied.

"And to feel heard, what would that mean?" Dr. Riley asked.

"It would mean that he listened empathetically. Instead of saying, well everyone experiences that. Or telling me what to do to fix the situation, I want him to just say, I'm sorry this is happening to you."

"Can you give an example?" Dr. Riley prompted her.

"Sure. Last week, I was frustrated because the kids' orthodontist was running late, and I had a meeting with the new development I was doing PR for. When I told Daniel that night what happened, he went into a whole speech on how I should always book the first appointment of the day for the kids so that I wouldn't run into the same problem again."

"Did you need him to do that?" Dr. Riley asked.

"No. I know how to problem solve. What I wanted him to say was, 'I'm sorry that your day was rough,' or something like that," Heather replied.

"And when Daniel always has an answer, how does that make you feel?"

"Like he doesn't trust me to figure it out. I kind of feel like he doesn't think I'm smart enough," Heather replied with a shaky voice. Dr. Riley could sense that this was a pain point for her.

"Do you see how this is affecting Heather?" Dr. Riley asked Daniel.

"I do now," Daniel said. He hadn't been aware that his actions affected Heather so deeply.

"Do you understand what you could do to help?" Dr. Riley asked.

"I'll definitely try to listen more. And I'll try to not always have the solution," Daniel added. "But I know that'll be hard. That's how I was raised. My dad always had the answer."

"And how was his relationship with your mom?"

"Fine. I guess. I mean they're still married after nearly fifty years, but they certainly bickered. And she tended to get mad at him a lot," Daniel paused as it dawned on him. "She probably felt like you do now," Daniel finished as he turned to Heather.

"I love your parents," Heather said. "But I don't want the relationship they have."

"Me neither," Daniel replied.

"Look, you guys are working on your relationship. You should absolutely recognize that you each have a different way of dealing with things based on how you grew up, but that doesn't mean you have to follow those same patterns."

"That's a relief," Daniel said. Heather smiled. While they both came from loving families, they each had their quirks and Heather preferred the way she and Daniel related to each other over anything she'd seen in any of their parents.

"Okay, Daniel, so now that you see the problem, can you work on it and try to refrain from giving solutions? Instead, just listen and be in the conversation?"

"I'm definitely going to try," Daniel responded. "But I might need some reminding."

"I'm happy to do that," Heather said then added. "And, look, I'm not innocent in this either. I need to work on my listening skills too. Since he always seems to have an answer, I've gotten in the habit of ignoring him. And because I don't know when he's flexing his muscle or actually trying to help, I just tune him out. Which, obviously, is not good."

"That's an incredible observation," Dr. Riley said as he put his pen and notepad down with a smile. He enjoyed these moments when the couples he worked with reached these kinds of realizations. Heather and Daniel were smiling for the first time since they walked into his room that day.

"By the way," Dr. Riley said. "This issue of men not listening empathetically is a common complaint women have about their marriage. It's a source of great unhappiness and frustration for women. They often say they don't feel heard or really listened to and that their husbands are too quick to try and just give them a solution. But the men aren't doing it on purpose. It's really due to gender differences in the way society socially conditions men with such a high priority on primarily just being good problem solvers. It doesn't teach them how to be better listeners nor how to actually be empathetic when they are listening while society generally does so for women."

"See, it's not completely my fault," Daniel laughed.

"I know, and I know you're trying," Heather replied with a smile.

"You both are doing a great job. I think we've reached a point where we can end today's session. Can you agree to spend the next week working on this together?" Dr. Riley asked.

Heather and Daniel both nodded and agreed to continue their work at home. They vowed to work with each other to be specific about their needs and to point out when they were feeling frustrated.

~~~

"Where is your father?" Kulap asked Kevin as they stood in the kitchen preparing dinner. Pilar was helping.

"Work?" Kevin guessed with a shrug of his shoulders.

"No, I called his producer, Ryan. He finished an hour and a half ago," Kulap replied as she slapped on an apron.

"Maybe he's with Chet," Pilar added as she opened the oven.

"What makes you think that?" Kulap asked.

"Chet came by earlier and asked if I wanted to go to happy hour," Pilar said. "I told him I could go tomorrow but tonight I had to help around here."

"Well, it's good to know someone kept their spousal promise," Kulap replied.

"Not sure it was worth it," Pilar said as she pulled a pan full of charred lumps out of the oven. She turned to Kevin. "Can't you do anything right?" she quipped as she threw the contents of the pan into the trash. Kevin recoiled at the sight.

Pilar's comment had struck a nerve in him. Even though he'd talked to his dad about them living in the house, he knew her shoving the burnt rolls in the trash was a passive aggressive dig at the way he operated in the world. Kevin tried to shrug it all off, but that night, the scene in the Riley house was chaotic to say the least. The tension wasn't just between Kevin and Pilar. The pressure had been building all afternoon.

Kevin was mad at Nola for using up all the hot water during her pre-dinner shower. "Don't you have any respect for others?" Kevin threw out the general accusation because he himself was feeling disrespected by his own wife.

Nola was mad at George for bringing home a slice of pecan pie from the grocery store but not letting her eat it all at once. "It's bad for your blood sugar," George had said. "You're growing a human, can't you be more responsible?"

"You can't control me," Nola had responded. Nola was upset because if there were anyone who was irresponsible it was George, not her.

George was annoyed with Kulap because she had kicked her out of the kitchen. "This is my domain," Kulap had said. "When you pay rent, you can take over." That comment had offended George who knew Nola was already worried about their financial situation.

And now Kulap was upset with Dr. Steve because she'd discovered he'd gone out and had a drink with Chet and forgot to call her. She left him a message on his cell, "I'm here with your family and you get to go out and have fun?"

No one was being specific about what they needed in those moments. Any Love Needs that had been established in any of their relationships had clearly been neglected.

Dinner was finally ready and Kulap was ready to eat. "Sit, sit. Everyone sit," she demanded. The family took their respective seats at the dinner table. Dr. Steve's spot was empty.

"We can start without him," Kulap said as she began to pass the salad around.

Just then Dr. Steve arrived. "I'm here. Sorry I'm late," he said as he leaned down to give Kulap a quick kiss on the cheek. She turned her head. Dr. Steve felt the chilly welcome. He could feel the tension in everyone.

"You know what this dinner needs?" he asked as he walked over to the wine fridge and held up a bottle of Merlot. "A little toast."

"You're gonna open that one?" Kulap exclaimed. "I thought we were saving it for a special moment."

"What's more special than dinner with the whole family?" Dr. Steve said.

"I think there's going to be a lot of those now that everyone's living here," Kulap retorted. Though Kulap loved Dr. Steve's family, having them all there was stressful. One of her Love Needs was feeling like she was a part of the Riley family, but since Dr. Steve had been so busy with work lately, she didn't feel like she had his support with the kids and their spouses.

Pilar sensed the anger in Kulap and glared at Kevin. "I told you we should've moved into the dorms," Pilar said under her breath.

Dr. Steve heard her and responded. "No one needs to live anywhere else. You're all welcome here. Right, Kulap?"

"Sure," Kulap replied as she grabbed the bottle of wine and poured herself a large glass. When they had discussed her Love Need of feeling like a part of the family, Dr. Steve had expressed his desire for her to have a genuine relationship with his kids. This was something they had agreed to work on together. In that moment, however, she was frustrated with him and knew that taking a few sips of wine would be better for everyone than if she spoke her mind.

"I think maybe we need to talk about some things," Dr. Steve said.

"Are you turning dinner into a therapy session?" George asked excitedly. She'd been trying to corner Dr. Steve for a while now to get help with her relationship with Nola. "Because I really think Nola and I need to work on being more specific when we talk about our Love Needs."

"It's absolutely important to determine specifically what each of you need to feel more deeply loved," Dr. Steve said. "I was just working with some clients today on this. We can walk through it if you want."

"No thanks, we'll pass," Nola said. Nola knew that she needed to talk to George about what being responsible looked like and how that would make her feel loved and secure, but she did not want to talk about it at the dinner table.

"Are you sure you don't want to talk?" Dr. Steve asked.

"Trust me, we know what to do," Nola said. "We're totally up to date on your podcasts and George even taped a quote from your book on our mirror."

"The solution for so many relationship problems would seem to be so incredibly clear, why don't we make the purpose of romantic relationships and marriage to be the mutual fulfillment of Love Needs? Doesn't everyone deserve to be loved in the ways that they need to feel truly happy?" George said, quoting the book verbatim.

Dr. Steve was impressed. "Thank you, George," Dr. Steve replied. "It's nice to know it's helping you."

"We've been listening to your podcast too," Pilar said. "And Kevin and I have been working on communicating our Love Needs to each other."

"Working is the operative word here," Kevin said. While he and Pilar had discussed their own Love Needs, they were still figuring out how to clearly articulate them to each other.

"Nothing's perfect overnight," Dr. Riley added. "Look at the two of us," Dr. Steve said as he placed his hand gently on top of Kulap's. Kulap was about to pull away, but then Dr. Steve continued, "We're good, but we still have to work on communicating what we both want from each other."

Kulap finally softened as she often did when Dr. Steve spoke with such calm authority. They had reached a point in their relationship where they could get upset with one another, but also knew how to quickly de-escalate their conflicts.

"I'm sorry I didn't let you know that I was going to hang with Chet for a bit," Dr. Steve said.

"I could've been clear when I said I wanted you to come home early tonight," Kulap began, "I should've stated that I needed your help with dinner. That I wanted it to be a family activity."

"Yes," Dr. Steve started, "But I could've called and told you I'd be late."

"Normally, you know I wouldn't have cared," Kulap replied. "But there's a lot happening around here these days."

Dr. Steve nodded his head. "I think we're all adjusting to this new normal and it's a good example of what happens when we fail to articulate our needs: we end up frustrated."

"That's a very good reminder, sir," George said. "Right, Nola?" Nola nodded but it was clear the conversation had made her think more deeply about her own needs within her marriage.

"Yeah, Dad, thanks," Kevin added. "Can we eat now?"

"Yes. Let's eat," Dr. Steve said. "I'm glad we all had this talk. I hope all of us continue to communicate what we need," Dr. Steve said as he raised his glass and smiled at the family.

"You can count me in," George said as she raised her glass and tapped it to Dr. Steve's.

~~~

After dinner, Nola and George retired to their room. Nola was pacing back and forth in front of the bed. George was scrolling through her phone reading marijuana recipes.

"Did you know you can make edibles out of anything? You think I should start a new business?" George asked.

"No. Absolutely not," Nola replied. "We moved here to get a jumpstart on a real life as a family. You can't be selling marijuana laced goodies out of my dad's house."

"I wouldn't sell them out of his house. I could get a little shop somewhere," George said optimistically.

"Where, George? Is that a well-thought-out business plan that's going to reassure me?"

"I don't know. I would figure it out," George said. "I want you to be happy."

"Do you know what would make me happy, George? If you figured out a real job," Nola said.

"Oh, so that's what all your comments were about at dinner tonight. Should we talk about it?" George said. "Seems to me like there's a Love Need not being fulfilled."

"Could you try not to mimic him, please?" Nola loved her dad and trusted in his process, but it annoyed her when George tried to play therapist.

"I just like the way he talks with such confidence," George replied. Nola glared at her. "But this is between you and me, so let's talk wife to wife. You clearly want me to get a job."

"Yes, but not because I want fancy things. I want financial security and right now, we don't have it," Nola said.

"So, we have some debt. But we have a roof over our heads," George pointed out.

"My dad's roof. Which is fine. But, remember what we said when we came here? This isn't forever," Nola said. Throughout their five-day journey from Los Angeles to Minnesota George and Nola had discussed their future. They had made a plan that they would use their stay at Dr. Steve's house to pay off their debts and get back on their feet.

"I thought our plan was to take a couple years," George said.

"And I think that's where I wasn't clear. I don't want to live off my dad that long. I don't want to sit around. I want us to be proactive," Nola said.

"And by us you mean me," George pointed out.

"I would get a job too, but I don't know who's going to hire someone who's seven months pregnant," Nola replied.

"I think that's discrimination," George said. Nola gave her a look that said that wasn't the point. "But I see how you need me to step up and be the responsible one right now."

"You do?" Nola asked. Nola was surprised that George had caught on so quickly.

"Of course. You have a lot to worry about already. I can't even imagine what it's like to be pregnant and the amount of pressure that brings. I mean, I feel it as a mom already and that baby isn't even inside me," George revealed.

Nola softened. Having George finally admit that she also felt pressure to be a good parent made her feel less alone in the journey. "I didn't know you felt that way," she said.

"Are you kidding me? I'm completely scared. And, this is no excuse, but that's probably why I haven't been so on top of things lately. When I get scared, I make bad choices," George said.

Nola laughed. "Yes, but I still love you. I just need you to do better. I need you to step up and help me."

"I want to find a job. I want to support you and us and the baby. I do. In fact, I'll start looking tomorrow. Or even right now."

George picked up her phone and started Googling local jobs. Nola felt a sense of relief to watch George take immediate action. Even though George had always been a good listener, George wasn't always so good at following through. Watching her scroll through job opportunities made her see that when she asked specifically for what she needed George would step up to the plate.

"I appreciate this," Nola started then placed George's hand gently on her belly and said, "And we thank you."

George paused at the word *we*, then realized... "Oh my god, I can feel a kick," George exclaimed. Nola smiled. Though their life wasn't perfect, it was pretty great and with a little work on both of their parts she knew it could be even better. "I could fall asleep to this every night."

"I actually do," Nola said as she placed her hand over George's hand and closed her eyes.

~~~

The next morning, Kevin drove Pilar to her first day of school at Macalester University.

"Are we good?" Kevin asked.

"Yeah," Pilar said. "Why wouldn't we be?"

"I just wanted to make sure, because of that comment you made last night," Kevin said. "About us living at my dad's."

"It was an awkward moment with Kulap. I felt like she didn't want us there. But after her and your dad talked it out, I feel better," Pilar said.

"You know how she is. She means well, she's just not always that welcoming," Kevin said as he pulled into the parking lot of school.

"I know," Pilar said. "I think I was nervous about starting school and it made me worry about our future. I mean, we went from having our own place in an amazing city to living with your dad and stepmom. That's a little awkward for two adults who are almost thirty, don't you think?"

"Absolutely. And that's why I was going to check out some of the continuing ed classes here," Kevin said.

"You are? For what?" Pilar asked.

"I don't know. I was thinking something creative might be good. I already got that job at the Pink House so I figured that when I wasn't waiting tables I could work on my business plan for the dinner theatre," Kevin said.

"That's really ambitious," Pilar said. She knew about Kevin's dreams, but it had been a while since she'd actually seen him take action on them. In D.C., he worked all the time to keep up with his share of the financial responsibilities but seeing him get back to his passion made her happy. "I like hearing that," she continued. "It's been awhile since I've seen you get excited about something that was for you."

"Is it okay?" he asked timidly. He had committed to supporting her dream of earning a PhD, but they hadn't really talked about what his role would be in Minnesota.

"You don't have to ask me permission," she said.

"I know but I thought that you needed me to be our financial rock during this time. You made that clear when we discussed our Love Needs," he said.

"I did. But I also want you to have what you need too. Look, we're living with your dad and Kulap to save money. You've got a job. I don't see why you can't do something for yourself," Pilar said.

Kevin put the car in park then leaned over and kissed Pilar on the forehead. "I'm really lucky I married you," he said.

"Me too," she replied. "Now go enroll in something fun and I'll see you back here at three."

As Pilar walked off towards Handel Hall for her first class, Kevin walked through campus on a high. He and Pilar were on the same page and both understood fully how to support each other and provide the kind of love the other needed. He was excited to finally have this time to not only work on his dreams but also to do it with Pilar by his side while she worked on her dreams.

~~~

Dr. Steve arrived home from his regular morning run an hour after he'd began. As he slowly made his way up the driveway, he thought about how last night, after dinner, he and Kulap had briefly discussed their conversation at the table. They had agreed to continue to work harder to meet each other's Love Needs, but Dr. Steve knew they still needed to delve further into the specifics of what they both needed now that the dynamic at home had changed.

Just as he had this thought, the garage door opened.

Dr. Steve paused and waited to see which kid or in-law would step out, but he was pleasantly surprised to find Kulap standing in the middle of the room wearing nothing but an oversized "Macalaster College" sweatshirt.

"Surprise!" Kulap said with her arms stretched wide.

Dr. Steve gave Kulap a seductive once over then took in his surroundings as he entered the garage.

"I'm not sure what surprise is better," Dr. Steve started. "You, wearing this? Or this room?"

"It's not just a room. It's your office," Kulap responded.

After watching Dr. Steve try to manage his work from the kitchen table amidst the chaos of the house, Kulap had decided that Dr. Steve needed his own space again. Kevin had helped her move Dr. Steve's desk and bookcase upstairs from the office. She had then arranged the books alphabetically, except for Dr. Steve's book which she had placed front and center on the first shelf. On the top shelf she had placed their wedding photo and behind it on the wall was a painting of Humble Lake that they had purchased at a local art fair. She'd even managed to paint the walls a beautiful blue so that it really felt like an office and not a garage.

"You didn't have to do this," Dr. Steve said.

"I know how busy you are with the podcast and your patients. I wanted you to have your own space," Kulap said. Though their home life had changed, Kulap still deeply understood that one of Dr. Steve's Love Needs was being supported in his work and she wanted him to feel that.

Dr. Steve appreciated how much Kulap championed his career ambitions. Though he was in his late fifties and many men his age had begun to plan their retirements, Dr. Steve had no plans to slow down. In fact, he was ramping his career up. The podcast was just the beginning. When he thought about his career, he saw more books, speaking engagements, and retreats for couples around the world to reconnect.

"This is really thoughtful," Dr. Steve said as he picked up their wedding photo and noticed all the details Kulap had paid attention to in his new office. "I don't really know what to say."

"I do," Kulap replied as she stood on her tiptoes and ran her fingers through his hair. Kulap knew that move made him go crazy. "Promise me you'll support me when I ask us to do things as a family."

"Of course, I will," Dr. Steve said. "I'm sorry again for going out with Chet last night. You know I want us to be a family together. And I know the situation is a little different with everyone living here, so clearly we need to communicate what we need."

"When I asked you to be home, it wasn't just for me it was for everyone," Kulap said.

"And I see that now. I had just assumed that things would be how they always were, but obviously it's not that easy and I'm glad you've pointed it out," Dr. Steve replied. They hadn't encountered this need before, back then they only saw the kids a few times a year and it was easy for him to support her relationship with the kids. But now that they were living together, she needed his constant support. "I will be more conscious of this," Dr. Steve said.

"Thank you," Kulap said as she softened. She loved the way Dr. Steve assured her that she was heard and that was all Kulap needed to feel better about the entire situation.

"This is going to be good for all of us," Dr. Steve said.

"I hope so," Kulap replied. "Because I'd hate to have wasted all that time on this amazing new office."

"It is pretty incredible," Dr. Steve said as he wrapped his arms around her and pushed the button on the garage door remote. As the door closed, he began to kiss Kulap.

Despite all that was going on with the kids and with Dr. Steve's career, their relationship was gaining strength with every conversation. Dr. Steve was happy that they had built a relationship where they could calmly and specifically address each other's needs. Kulap liked the way Dr. Steve really listened to her and came up with ways to take action. Both appreciated their time alone together.

"Now this is one of those moments I dreamed of when we bought this house," Kulap said in between kisses.

Chapter 5

Podcast #5
Underlying Resentment
Sabotages Love Needs!

"Chronic hurt and resentment from repeating conflict make it difficult to even want to step forward to meet love needs. There is a direct link between love needs not being met and degree of conflict. Stored-up feelings of hurt and resentment from repeating patterns of conflict may cause a buildup of subconscious resistance.

It's natural to feel like we don't want to go out of our way to meet the needs of partners when feeling hurt or angry. The more negative feelings there are, the more resistance there is to act unselfishly towards a partner. It can be hard for one to show openness and interest in meeting each other's love needs if there are underlying negative feelings. This is especially true if we're upset over our own needs not being met!

Thus, freeing up your relationship to better meet love needs may depend on how well you and your partner learn to handle conflict!"

"We hit a roadblock this week," Daniel Green said as Heather nodded in agreement.

The Greens were back in Dr. Riley's office. They had returned for their fifth session and were reporting on their progress. They had worked on being specific when they talked about their Love Needs, but there was an underlying sense of not wanting to follow through. After listening to Dr. Riley's fifth podcast episode, they understood that there was more going on than they were admitting to each other.

"I feel stuck," Heather said. "Daniel's been trying to listen to me and my needs but it doesn't feel like he's really interested in me as a person. I keep feeling like it's not enough. Even when he does what I ask, I still have a negative reaction to it."

"There's this disbelief with her," Daniel started. "Even when I say or do something that she's asked me to do, she doesn't think I'm being truthful. Like, the other day. She asked if I respected her and I said, of course, how could I not? She's the mother of our children."

"Yeah, but it didn't feel genuine," Heather said.

"But it was," Daniel replied.

"Let's back it up a bit," Dr. Riley said before the two could continue bickering. He had seen this pattern before. "I'm sensing some hidden resentment behind what you're saying Heather."

"That's part of it," Heather said. She knew that deep down Daniel had a certain kind of love for her, but often felt that he didn't really respect her. He was constantly talking over her, interrupting her. To Heather it seemed like he was trying to prove his worth by dominating the conversation. Heather didn't need him to do this. She knew her husband was smart and made great career and financial decisions for the family, but she didn't sign up to marry a know-it-all. Lately, however, that's all she got from him. "I worry that we're stuck in a pattern where he's always trying to push his own agenda. I feel like he has no real interest in me and honestly, I hate it and find myself more and more resentful," Heather finished.

"How does that make you feel, Daniel?" Dr. Riley asked.

"Well, I see her point. But I also get frustrated when she dismisses me so easily," Daniel added.

"I'm tired, Dr. Riley," Heather sighed. "All of our discussions end in the same standstill they always end in," Heather started. "I feel like Daniel's always trying to promote what he wants without really truly caring about what I want."

"And I feel like she's too critical. Like I can't do anything right," Daniel said. "It's like we're in a catch-22. I'm just trying to be helpful."

Dr. Riley laughed. "Let's talk about this.

"Okay, let me start," Daniel began, "I'm not trying to push any sort of agenda or prove I'm right. I'm a rational problem solver, so when Heather has a problem, I naturally want to help her This is what I do all day at work. It's just a natural extension of me. I truly just want to help her."

"Can you accept that this is his real intention behind what he's doing?" Dr. Riley asked Heather.

"Yes. But sometimes that feels too dominating in a way that makes me think he doesn't care about my feelings. He seems more interested in trying to fix the problem and move on, than listen to me."

"And when Daniel's help feels too dominating what happens?" Dr. Riley prompted her.

"I shut down. I don't want to talk or hear more," Heather admitted.

"Okay, so Daniel what if you simply listened first, then showed empathy, and asked questions allowing her to share more with you? Or, even asked her what she needed in these types of situations."

"I could do that," Daniel said.

"It would help me," Heather started calmly, "If you didn't always jump to a conclusion that you know best. Sometimes I know you do but first let me ask for your help. And ask me if I even need it or want it."

"That's a good way to put it," Dr. Riley said. "It seems to me that there's much you've avoided talking about because it was simply easier for Heather to stay quiet and move on. But as you can see that only leads to a buildup of hurt and resentment."

"I don't want that," Daniel added then turned to Heather. "So, can we work on this?"

Heather smiled and placed her hand on top of Daniel's. "Yes, absolutely."

"I think this is the perfect spot to stop for the day," Dr. Riley said. "I trust that you two will spend the next week working through any resentment that's built up."

"We definitely will," Daniel said.

~~~

After the Greens left, Dr. Riley stayed behind to continue working. The Greens were his last clients that day and he had asked Ryan to join him that afternoon to work on the podcast.

Kulap had also brought him lunch and decided to stay and hang out. They often did this before the move. Kulap would bring a book and read while Dr. Riley worked on his podcast. When he needed a break, they would take walks around the neighborhood together or if it was late enough grab a glass of wine. This was the part of their relationship that Kulap had been looking forward to having more of. When they married, she took an early retirement from her career as a Xerox sales executive. Together they had decided that they wanted to spend more time together. Since Kulap's work kept her on the road quite a bit, retirement was the best option to give her the freedom to enjoy life on the lake with her husband.

That day, Kulap had been fully engrossed in her book when she overheard Ryan telling Dr. Riley there was good news. Kulap perked up from her seat on the chaise lounge chair in the lobby and walked into Dr. Riley's office.

"What's going on?" she asked from the precipice of the room.

Ryan and Dr. Riley turned to Kulap. Dr. Riley motioned for her to come in and take a seat.

"Ryan was just about to give me the numbers from the first few podcast episodes," Dr. Riley said.

"That's exciting," Kulap replied. "So?"

"The numbers were great," Ryan began. "You've already had four hundred downloads."

"Does this mean we can celebrate?" Kulap asked.

"Not quite," Ryan replied. "That's a great number, but it's nothing to sneeze at yet."

"What would be a great number?" Kulap asked.

"In the thousands," Ryan replied.

"Thousands?" Dr. Riley gasped.

"Tens of thousands would be better," Ryan added.

"Is that possible?" Dr. Riley asked.

"With the right marketing strategy, absolutely," Ryan said.

"Okay, so what do we need to do?" Kulap asked. Though this wasn't Kulap's career, she felt like she had a one hundred percent stake in it, and she wanted her husband to succeed.

"We need to get you out there more on social media," Ryan replied as he turned to face Dr. Riley.

"I don't know the first thing about social media," Dr. Riley replied.

"It's a good thing I do then," Ryan said. "I already set up your Instagram account. And I've been posting quite a few things."

"What did you post?" Dr. Riley asked as he grabbed Ryan's phone and flipped through the Instagram app. In his feed were stock photos of happy couples with captions describing different principles of Relationship Co-Coaching and how they can lead to marital satisfaction. These photos were interspersed with anonymous quotes and excerpts from his book. "Oh, I like this."

"Great because we're going to go live," Ryan said.

"What does that mean?" Dr. Riley asked.

"It means I hit this button here and there's a live stream of video that plays to all of your followers," Ryan replied. "People do it to give their audience more of a sense of connection."

"Okay, so what? I just talk?" Dr. Riley asked.

"I was thinking it'd be kind of nice if you and Kulap went on there and discussed your relationship," Ryan said.

"I don't know. I'm fine with being the face of this movement as you say, but Kulap didn't sign up for this." Dr. Riley said. "She doesn't need to be involved if she doesn't want to."

"Hold on. I am totally fine being another face of this movement," Kulap began. "What's the point of spending thousands on proper facial care if no one gets to see how well I'm aging?" She smiled as she brushed her hand across her cheeks.

"You spend what?" Dr. Riley asked in shock. Kulap shrugged it off.

"Don't worry about it. Now it'll be a write off," she smiled. She then turned to Ryan. "So, what do we talk about on here?"

"Why don't you talk about your own relationship patterns and how Love Needs can get sabotaged sometimes. That'll dovetail nicely with this week's episode," Ryan said. "Oh, and, this way, Dr. Riley, by answering questions about your own relationship you can circumvent the ethical dangers you've shared of trying to solve caller's marital problems on the podcast without proper assessment beforehand and follow-up afterwards."

"Okay," Dr. Riley said. "Let's do it."

Ryan held the phone and pointed the video camera at Dr. Riley and Kulap.

Kulap brushed her hair away from her left cheek. "Make sure you're shooting my good side,"

"You look great," Ryan said. "You guys ready?"

Kulap smiled and Dr. Riley nodded. They began to talk about the early days of their relationship. The live stream of them talking was broadcast out to the world to see. Ryan had a pleased look on his face through the entire thing as people started to show up and watch them.

Questions soon appeared on the screen. Dr. Riley read one aloud. "How do you deal with knowing each other's needs but not always fulfilling them?" Dr. Riley's answer came right away. "Well, first, we work on being specific with what we need and want."

"And we try to gently let each other know when something bothers us," Kulap added.

"We've learned over time that we can't let any of our feelings fester," Dr. Riley said then continued. "This is something I tell all my clients. When you first start to discuss your Love Needs there's often resistance because there's built up resentment that gets in the way. But if you can talk through what you're angry or resentful about and resolve it then things can be better."

"True. But this definitely doesn't happen overnight," Kulap added into the camera.

"Of course not. This takes work for everyone. And that's because no one ever warned any of us that after the early phase of romantic infatuation, even in really great relationships, we should expect to frequently say and do things to hurt each other's feelings. We're all imperfect."

"What do you always tell me?" Kulap added. "That it's perfectly normal to unintentionally hurt your partner's feelings and it should be expected.

Sometimes even once every day or two or sometimes more when under particularly stressful situations." Kulap then continued. "And that we have to address and heal these feelings so that they don't build and harm the relationship."

"Exactly," Dr. Riley said as he gave her an affectionate look. "We are all deeply emotional human beings who can be easily slighted and hurt by those we love so deeply. If we don't address these feelings hurt and resentment builds."

"It sure does," Kulap revealed.

"She's right. But I never mean to hurt Kulap and the same goes for her. She never means to hurt me. But it happens. And when it does, we try to address it immediately."

Kulap nodded in agreement. "I used to get so mad at him when we were going out to a nice dinner and I'd ask, 'how do I look?' And he'd say, 'you look nice.' I would look at him like, 'What does that even mean?'" Kulap finished as Dr. Riley smiled at the memory.

"It didn't dawn on me that she wanted to hear more than "nice"," Dr. Riley added.

"But, as you found out, I need more feedback when it comes to my appearance," Kulap said.

"I know. And I also now know that you genuinely wanted my honest opinion."

"Exactly. I wanted you to look at me and if I looked good, I wanted you to say, 'you look great.' And if something looked off, I wanted you to say, 'why don't you try that other dress I love so much.' I really want to know what you think."

"But I didn't see that at first. Instead, I viewed your question as a trap and tried to avoid it. But once we really talked about what we each meant, it was clear that neither of us was trying to hurt the other."

"I remember feeling such a relief when we got to the bottom of that," Kulap sighed.

"Me too," Dr. Riley added.

"I will say that working through things like this has definitely helped us. We don't have as many hurt feelings or as much resentment under the surface anymore," Kulap said.

"True," Dr. Riley said.

"And how do I look today?" Kulap asked with a flourish of her hands.

"Gorgeous," Dr Riley replied. He then turned to the camera and spoke directly to his audience. "The problem I see couples have is that when they feel hurt by their partner, they don't say anything. But you can't ignore these feelings. Because when you suppress them for too long internal pressure builds up and then those feelings burst as anger and rise to the surface and conflict begins. If you stay in this pattern, vitality is sucked from the relationship, and over time it can severely damage love feelings."

"And who wants that?" Kulap said with a shrug and a lift of her hands. The likes and comments on the live stream kept rolling through. Ryan continued to cheer them on silently from behind the camera and Dr. Riley felt like he was on point.

"No one," Dr. Riley said as he leaned over and kissed his wife. He felt very good about how great she was teaming up with him on camera. Though they had worked through these issues in the past, talking through them on Instagram live served as a reminder of how far they'd come in their relationship and how much they had learned to let go of resentment. Also, they now knew how to prevent it.

Ryan slowly faded out the live video on the image of the happy couple—Dr. and Mrs. Riley.

"That was incredible," Ryan said as he put down the phone. "You guys were great! People were loving it. We will definitely be doing this again."

"I can agree to that," Dr. Riley said. "As long as my co-host is by my side."

"Okay. But next time I'm getting my hair done first," Kulap said.

"Deal," Dr. Riley replied.

Kulap smiled. She would happily help her husband any chance she had, plus she liked that they were able to revisit their own issues on camera. She could see how it would benefit them both immensely. As Dr. Riley had always made clear, the more a couple shared their Love Needs in specific terms and talked about the patterns that lead to resentment, the more they could enjoy each other.

"I think this going live thing will be good for us," Kulap said.

"Me too," Dr. Riley agreed.

~~~

The next morning, Kevin awoke to find Pilar snoring next to him. He smiled at the sweet sound she made as she breathed in and out. Kevin gently kissed her on the forehead and slid out of bed. She had an hour before she needed to be up for school, and he didn't want to wake her. He quietly donned a pair of sweats and a t-shirt and headed upstairs

Kevin was in search of a hot cup of coffee but when he got to the kitchen he wasn't greeted by the smell of roasted beans, instead he was greeted by an extremely distinct smell. Kevin took a few short inhales through his nose as if he was a greyhound sniffing out the scent of a predator, then determined that the scent was coming from outside. He made his way to the sliding glass door off the side of the kitchen that led to the wraparound patio that surrounded the entire back of the house. As he stepped outside, he quickly found the source of the smell. It was George standing at the railing, looking out over the lake. She turned at the sound of Kevin stepping onto the wood planks of the porch. Kevin nodded hello and George gave him a smile as she placed a joint to her lips and inhaled deeply.

"I thought I smelled something out here," Kevin said.

George pulled the joint away from her lips then slowly exhaled. "You want some?" she asked as she held up the joint for Kevin.

Kevin hesitated for a moment. He hadn't smoked marijuana since before he and Pilar got married, and even then, he'd never liked the way it made him feel. When D.C. legalized the drug, he and Pilar had eaten a few edibles to try it out, but it wasn't something they did regularly. Pilar didn't like to be out of control, and she felt like she never could predict how she'd react to the THC. Kevin on the other hand, liked the unpredictability of life, but always felt he had to tame that side of himself around Pilar. Today, however, he felt differently. Things were good with him and Pilar.

"You know what?" Kevin said as he took the joint from George. "I think I'll have some."

Kevin took a deep inhale then tried to hold his breath but began to cough. "Wow, that's strong," he said.

"I know, I grew it," George said proudly.

"Really? Where?" Kevin asked.

"Back in LA. I had my own little farm there," George replied.

"You had a farm in Los Angeles? Where did you find space for that? Last time I visited Nola she barely had a window sill," Kevin responded.

"Well, I took a soundstage and turned it into an indoor grow room," George replied.

"That's legal?" Kevin asked.

"Not exactly," George replied with a sullen face.

"So that's how you ended up here?" Kevin asked.

"Something like that," George said. "I wish I had just filed the correct permits and asked for permission to use the space. Nola still won't let it go."

"Have you talked to her?" Kevin asked.

"Of course," George replied. "And she says she's forgiven me, but it doesn't feel like it."

"Let me guess," Kevin said. "She'll be fine and then something will remind her of the one thing you did that made her mad and suddenly she's talking about how you never listen."

"Exactly," George sighed. "I always think I'm doing the right thing and meeting her needs, and then something goes wrong. I've got a job interview today because I know she wants me to be more reliable."

"I'm sure she appreciates that," Kevin said.

"See that's the thing. I'm not sure it's enough. I have this fear that she's going to want me to make more money, or it won't be the right job, or there'll be something else I'm doing that's not responsible enough," George sighed. "You know, I'm trying to be a good wife, but it's hard."

"I'm sure you are," Kevin replied. "Nola's not always easy."

"She is though. That's why I love her," George said wistfully. Kevin knew exactly what George was talking about. Nola was the peacemaker in the family.

"I know Nola's not one for confrontation, but I'd talk to her" Kevin said. "Ask her what she really needs right now. Things change and I'm sure she needs a lot more now that there's a baby on the way."

"You have a point, I need to keep talking to her."

"It's what my dad always tells everybody to do and it seems to work for Pilar and me," Kevin said as he took another drag from the joint. "And you have to make sure you clear the air on anything from the past."

"That sounds wise. Guess I got to heal some old wounds," George finished.

"You're sounding like my old man already," Kevin said. "And you've only been here a couple weeks."

"What can I say? I respect him," George replied.

"Me too," Kevin said as he exhaled the smoke from his lungs. "I'm pretty proud of him."

George took the joint back from Kevin and inhaled deeply. "Do you think he likes me?" she asked.

"You're married to my sister. He has to," Kevin replied as he gave George a good old slap on the back. "You're family now."

~~~

In the kitchen, Pilar found Nola sitting by herself sipping on a small cup of coffee.

"Oh good. I'm glad you're here," Pilar said.

"Don't know where else I'd be," Nola quipped as she pointed to her growing belly.

"That's exactly why I was hoping we could have a moment alone. I got to know," Pilar said. "How'd it all happen? Anonymous donor?"

Nola looked up from her mug. "I'd say he's anything but anonymous," Nola said proudly. "But we are keeping it a secret."

"I knew it. He's a Hollywood star," Pilar laughed. "Kevin and I were guessing."

"I wouldn't say star," Nola replied with a smile. This made Pilar intrigued.

"But he's someone we probably all know?" Pilar asked.

"Maybe," Nola said as she patted her belly with a wink.

"Okay, I like this game," Pilar said with a nod. "And I also respect your need for privacy.

Still, I can't believe you're having a baby," Pilar exclaimed as she opened her arms to hug Nola.

"I know. It's surreal," Nola said. "Kevin's going to be an awesome uncle, though."

Pilar smiled. Though she often felt that Kevin was too soft and not commanding enough Kevin did have a way with kids. Sometimes she wanted him to grow up, but often she loved him exactly for the way that he didn't submit to societal standards to be a man, follow a set career path and leave his wife at home to do the cooking, cleaning, and rearing of the children. When she and Kevin finally did decide to have kids, Pilar knew that she would be fully supported in any choice she made. And that Kevin would be an amazing stay-at-home dad, if that's what they might choose to do.

"Congrats on the wedding, too," Pilar said as she poured herself a cup of coffee.

"Thanks, I'm still adjusting to being a wife. It's good," Nola replied. Then, upon further reflection, "But you know with all this talk about relationship communication and not having any unexpressed negative feelings, I think I might have some."

George would get a job sure, but she knew that they had more to work through. She knew she needed to discuss her own resentment that kept bubbling up and caused her to still distrust George. Having George lose her job over an illegal pot farm was a big deal, and Nola feared George would do something reckless again. "I think George and I have a lot more to talk about."

"Isn't that what relationships are these days? It seems like that's all Kevin and I do," Pilar said. "Probably has something to do with living here."

"My dad does have that effect," Nola said with a smile.

Chapter 6

Podcast #6
Breaking the Cycle of NRP Conflict
with Softly Specific^{SM} Co-Coaching!

"Conflict typically starts in this way: one partner may express some concerns or important feelings to the other but feels frustrated when he or she becomes 'defensive,' 'doesn't listen,' 'interrupts,' or gets 'angry' (common NRPs). Then, a back-and-forth disagreement ensues, escalating rapidly. Does this sound familiar in your relationship?

This seems to be the universal cycle for conflict—hard to stop once it takes off. Or there may be *covert conflict* resulting in uncomfortable silent tension from buildup of negative feelings. Whether overt or covert, it saps the positive-romantic feelings and vitality from your relationship. Let's explore how to stop or reduce conflict using Softly Specific Co-Coaching^{SM}."

"Our fight wasn't that bad," Heather said to Dr. Riley. "But it also wasn't good. We worked hard on the resentment that's built over the years, but we still keep snapping at each other."

The Greens had arrived at Dr. Riley's for their sixth session. Though they were happy with their progress they still felt like they were hitting bumps in the road, like they couldn't escape the conflict that'd been there for years.

"I really thought we were getting somewhere with these sessions, but I don't know, I guess old habits die hard," Daniel added.

"It's not that old habits die hard," Dr. Riley began, "It's more that we live in a society that's never showed us how to handle conflict correctly."

"I mean conflict is definitely where we've been running into problems," Daniel said.

Dr. Riley nodded then explained, "In business, in politics, in every other life circumstance when we're upset, we let frustration build and build until it finally spews out and comes out in generalizations of global criticism which puts everyone on the defensive. When you had your fight, what did you say to each other?"

"I told him that he never helps around the house," Heather said.

"And I replied that I always help around the house," Daniel said in a raised tone. "Who takes out the trash and does the yard work?"

"You do," Heather said softly.

"But that's not enough?" Daniel scoffed.

Dr. Riley paused for a beat to let the air clear then asked, "It sounds to me like Heather's statement saying you *never* helped put you on the defensive?"

"Absolutely," Daniel said. "How could I sit there and not defend myself when what she was saying wasn't true."

This riled Heather. She sat up taller then said, "But the argument wasn't about that. The argument was about the fact that I'd asked him to cook dinner and when I got home from work, nothing was ready or even remotely prepared."

"I'd texted you to see what you wanted," Daniel said. "And when you said burgers, I said I needed you to pick up some meat and buns on the way home."

"But that's not the point. When I ask you to cook dinner, I want you to do everything that goes along with it. When I cook dinner, I don't call and ask you what you want and then tell you to go to the store and buy all the ingredients. I just handle it."

"Which is why I didn't think it was that big of a deal to ask you to pick up a few things. I was still going to cook," Daniel said defensively.

"I know, but by that point I'd already done seventy-five percent of the work," Heather said as she crossed her arms over her chest. "I might as well have done it myself."

"Well, that would avoid more fights," Daniel stated as he threw up his hands.

"Okay. Hold on," Dr. Riley began. "Giving up and giving in isn't going to solve this problem."

"I know," Daniel relented. "But sometimes this feels like a lot of work."

"It doesn't have to be," Dr. Riley said. "To change repeating conflict like this, it requires ongoing feedback from both of you. We all need helpful advice to change our behaviors. That's why I developed the Softly Specific co-coaching approach for couples."

"How does that work?" Heather asked.

"Co-coaching is basically coaching each other on how to change key behaviors and patterns of conflict. And the rest is kind of like it sounds. You must work on being soft and not aggressive when you ask for a change in behavior and be specific at the same time."

Daniel and Heather shifted in their seats and looked to Dr. Riley to explain further.

"So, Heather, instead of getting angry and raising your voice and telling Daniel that he doesn't do any work around the house. You start with calmly stating what bothered you specifically and how it made you feel relative to the vulnerable feelings underneath the anger."

"That sounds easy enough," Heather said. "I felt disrespected when you didn't take the time to fully plan and prepare dinner."

"Good," Dr. Riley said. "You also have to remember to be specific in requesting what you'd like in the future."

Heather turned to Daniel. "When I ask you to cook dinner, I need you to come up with a plan on your own. Tonight, I will eat anything but pork and I need you to do all the shopping that goes along with dinner. Like that?" Heather finished.

"Exactly," Dr. Riley said.

"If she put it that way every time, I could easily do everything she asked," Daniel added then turned to Heather as he realized. "I'm sorry I didn't put all of that together before."

"Apology accepted," Heather said as she turned to her husband and saw that he was genuinely apologetic. She felt like she was being heard for the first time in a long time and a sense of relief washed over her. She had put a lot of emotional labor into so many of the tasks around the house, and it was nice to finally see Daniel recognize that cooking dinner required more than just the cooking.

"Do you see how being specific about what you need helps the other understand better?" They both nodded yes. "And can you see how coaching each other along will help you to stop some of these patterns that have you both frustrated?"

"Absolutely," Heather replied. "I really thought we were fundamentally broken, but this is just a lot of miscommunication."

"Which we're going to work on together," Daniel said as he placed his hand over hers in a gesture of love. Heather interlaced her fingers with his and smiled. They had work to do, but now it felt doable.

~~~

Two weeks into life at the Riley lake house with the whole family, and everyone had begun to adjust to the situation. It was eight a.m. on a breezy Monday and all the kids were bustling through the kitchen getting ready to start their days.

"This is what I like to see," Dr. Steve said as he entered from the back patio. Dr. Steve had just completed his morning run and the sight of his two children and their spouses getting along with each other made him happy. If he'd ever imagined his whole family under one roof as adults, this is what he would've imagined. Of course, he hadn't done that because what parent imagines their late twenty-something kids moving back in with them? But that didn't mean he didn't like it.

As Dr. Steve made his way into the room, Kulap was already in the kitchen. When the Riley children first arrived, she had taken the time each morning to shower, do her hair, and dress as if she were going to work, but now she was comfortable with the situation just like everyone else and a comfy robe made perfect sense.

Breaking the Cycle of NRP Conflict with Softly SpecificSM
Co-Coaching!

71

"I made eggs," Nola said as Kulap approached the island in the middle of the kitchen. Nola was sitting at one of the two stools that faced out to the lake. George was next to her sipping a mug of coffee.

"Over easy?" Kulap asked and Nola nodded. "You remembered. They smell delicious," Kulap said as she grabbed a plate off the counter and made her way to the stovetop.

"Coffee's on the burner," Pilar added. She and Kevin were at the kitchen table where Dr. Steve had also taken a seat.

"Thirty more seconds and another English muffin will be popping up," George chimed in.

"You guys really have this morning routine covered, don't you?" Dr. Steve said as he hoisted his right ankle on top of his left thigh and leaned forward to engage in a post-run stretch.

"I like to call it a well-oiled machine," Kulap replied. "We've been working with each other to get this whole thing in sync." When the adult kids had first moved in, meals were complete chaos, but Kulap had been working with each one, coaching them on how she liked the mornings to go in her house.

"I can see that," Dr. Steve said as Kulap sat down at the table next to him with a plate full of food.

"Want some?" Kulap asked.

"Just a bite," Dr. Steve replied as he came up from his stretch. Kulap lifted a fork full of eggs to his lips. Dr. Steve took a bite with a smile. After he finished chewing, he went back to his stretches but continued talking. "What's everyone up to this week?"

"We're going to the doctor today," Nola said

"Seven-month check-up," George smiled. "Baby should be the size of a cauliflower head by now."

"So, you got a hold of Dr. McGrath?" Dr. Steve asked. The day after Nola arrived, Dr. Steve had asked a few of his friends and colleagues who the best obstetrician was in town these days and Dr. McGrath's name was the first on everyone's list.

"Yes. I did," Nola said as she gave George a sideways glance. George cowered because she was supposed to be in charge of making the appointment but had completely dropped the ball. Nola turned from George and back to her dad. "Did you know she used to work under Dr. Bray before he retired?" she asked.

Dr. Steve paused at the sound of Dr. Bray's name. Dr. Bray had delivered both Kevin and Nola and had taken incredible care of his wife Emily when she was pregnant. "I didn't know that," Dr. Steve said. "Awww, it makes me happy you're back here."

"Us too," George said. "It's going to be great raising our baby with family around. Right, Nola?"

Nola simply nodded and went back to her eggs. George felt the sting of the move. Dr. Steve noticed and thought about addressing it, but then Kulap began talking.

"What are you two up to?" she asked as she turned to Kevin and Pilar.

"First day of class today for me," Kevin said enthusiastically as he took a bite of her English muffin. "Theater 101."

"You're going to be an actor now?" Kulap asked.

"Of course not," Kevin said. "It's research for my dinner theater idea. Besides, I don't think I'm the one with the Hollywood gene in this family," Kevin added as he eyed Nola's growing baby bump. Pilar kicked him under the table.

"I think it's great you're taking classes. You know I got my doctorate when I was working," Dr. Steve said as he got up from the table and took Kulap's empty plate with him.

At the same time, George walked over to the counter to pour herself some more coffee and grabbed Nola's plate to scrape the uneaten bits into the garbage. As George pulled the overflowing trash bin from its rolling cabinet next to the sink she asked, "Whose turn is it to take out the trash?"

Nola, Kevin and Pilar all turned and shrugged.

"I thought we had a system here, guys," Kulap said. "Don't make me make a chore chart," Everyone turned to stare at her. "What? I never had kids. I always wanted to give out gold stars."

~~~

After the family had left the kitchen to begin their day, George found Dr. Steve in his garage office.

"Can I come in?" George asked as she gently knocked on the door.

Dr. Steve looked up from his desk. "Of course," he said then gestured for her to have a seat.

George plopped herself down. "I've got a problem, dad. And I know she's your daughter, but I also know you're a great therapist, so there's that."

"What can I help you with?" Dr. Steve said as he placed his full attention on George.

"I got a job," George started.

"That's great!" Dr. Steve exclaimed.

"Is it though? I went from producing movies to handling produce," George sighed.

"A job's a job, and I know you and Nola have some financial issues to deal with," Dr. Steve said. "But things will get better."

"I have hope they will. But that's why I'm here," George said. "I feel like I can't get anywhere with her. We've been listening to your podcast and using your techniques to get through a lot of our issues, but I feel like we're stuck. Like, I love and respect her, but we keep doing the same things to each other. I tell her I need her to trust me, and she tells me she needs me to be responsible. We both think we're doing what the other wants, but we both end up upset in the end."

Dr. Steve nodded his head up and down. He knew what George was talking about. He'd recently seen it with the Greens and had also seen it in all the couples he'd worked with over the last twenty years.

"Do you guys get frustrated with each other?"

"Yes," George said then thought about the fact that that's how every one of their fights ended.

"And when you're upset do you tell Nola calmly about your more vulnerable feelings underlying the anger or do you just express the anger in a way that is at least a little bit aggressive?"

George bowed her head then admitted, "It's more the latter."

Dr. Steve gave her a consoling look, then said, "It's nothing to be ashamed of. Not that I want you to be aggressive with my daughter, but it's commonplace in couples to let anger build up. Then when we get frustrated it comes out in ways we don't really mean."

"Yeah. I never mean to be rude about it, but by that point I'm always so mad," George said.

"Did you listen to this week's podcast?" Dr. Steve asked.

"The one about being soft and specific?" George asked.

Dr. Steve nodded yes.

"I try to be gentle with my words," George stated. "Though I'm sure I have an attitude here and there."

"It usually takes some time to get it right," Dr. Steve said. "But I have confidence you can figure it out. You still have my book, right?" George nodded. "Check out Chapter Four. It lays out exactly what you need to say."

"Okay," George said. "I can do that."

"Good," Dr. Steve said. "Now enjoy getting a glimpse of your baby. I used to love those appointments."

"I will," George said as she got up to leave.

"Wait. One more thing," Dr. Steve said. "Is it George Clooney?"

George gave Dr. Steve a puzzled look.

"The baby's father," Dr. Steve explained. "I overheard Pilar and Kevin making guesses the other day."

"No, sir, it's not. Think less chiseled jaw, more flowy hair," George said as she walked off leaving Dr. Steve to contemplate who the father could be.

~~~

At Dr. McGrath's office, George was caught up in the moment as she gushed over the sight of the baby on the ultrasound. "I'm so in love," George sighed. Nola smiled.

"Is it weird that all I want to do is sing Bon Jovi right now?" George asked as she started to play the air guitar and nod her head so that her hair flowed like the 80's rocker. "I'll be there for you, these five words I swear to you..." she harmonized.

Nola laughed an uncomfortable laugh. The doctor stared at her.

"I'm sorry. I'm just overwhelmed," George exclaimed as she squeezed Nola's hand. "The little one's like a real person now,"

"The little one? I'm assuming you don't know the sex then?" Dr. McGrath asked.

"No," Nola said.

"We want it to be a surprise," George added. "Also, Nola hates the idea of a gender reveal party." Back in LA they had considered throwing a party to find out the baby's sex for a brief moment but when they realized that they'd have to invite the baby's biological father and risk revealing his identity they had decided against it.

"Plus, we don't even live near any of our friends anymore. Who would come if we did it now?" Nola asked. The response was meant to be matter of fact, but it definitely came off passively aggressively. A slight to George and the fact that she was the reason they had to leave all their friends in Los Angeles behind. George felt it but didn't want the doctor to know all their business.

"Your family would come," George said. "Are you sure you don't want to know?"

"I'm sure," Nola replied. "We waited this long. We can wait a little longer." Nola said as she slipped her hand out from under George's and turned her eyes back to the screen. The baby's arms were moving back and forth across the screen.

"Is the baby waving?" George asked in an attempt to focus on the good of the moment and not the tension building between her and Nola.

"Might be," Dr. McGrath replied.

"I guess I'll take that as a sign to stay surprised," George said.

"Then it's decided," Dr. McGrath said. "I'll make a note in here that you are not finding out the sex before birth."

"So, that's it?" George asked.

"That's it. Nola is healthy. The baby is growing well. Everything is good," Dr. McGrath said. "Welcome to Minnesota."

"Well, that was easy," George said.

"For you," Nola replied.

After the doctor's appointment, George drove their Jeep straight to the nearest Culver's. Nola had insisted on going there. Her cravings had become strong in the last couple weeks and one of the things she had looked forward to about moving back home, was being able to order a ButterBurger. Though she liked the novelty of the In-N-Out burger in California, Nola had always had an affinity for Culver's since she was a kid playing soccer. Often, after each game her parents would take her and Kevin there for a special treat. While most kids wanted the frozen custard milkshake to go with the burger, Nola just wanted the burger.

They took their burgers back to the lake house and sat on the dock to enjoy them. George saw this quiet moment as an opportunity to discuss the issues she had brought up with Dr. Steve.

"I was hoping we could talk about some things," George said.

Nola took a big bite of her burger then nodded her head. This pleased George, but then she remembered something. "Great. Wait here," George said as she ran off to the house. A few minutes later she returned carrying Dr. Riley's book "Relationship Co-Coaching."

She sat down next to Nola and opened it to the section Dr. Steve had referenced that morning.

"Are you going to read me my dad's book?"

"No. I don't want to mess this up," George said. "I think it's important for our relationship."

Nola sighed. "Go on."

"I feel," George said then paused as she looked down at the page that was directing her how to offer feedback and request change in the Softly Specific method. She had reached the point where she was supposed to fill in the blank with non-angry vulnerable feelings such as hurt, afraid, disappointed, disrespected, sad, rejected, unloved. "I feel," she said again. "Disrespected when you make subtle passive-aggressive comments blaming me for our having to move to Minnesota like you did in the doctor's office and you don't acknowledge the positive things I'm doing when it comes to our finances."

"I know you're trying. I'm proud of you for getting that job at Whole Foods," Nola said.

"Wait, let me finish," George said. "This is where I'm supposed to request a specific behavior change."

"Okay," Nola said. She'd spent her entire young adulthood with her father, she knew it was her turn to listen.

"Would you please instead acknowledge the positive efforts I'm making and give me feedback respectfully about anything you're unhappy about. I need to know that the work I'm doing is what you want and need. Can you do this for me from now on?"

Nola thought for a moment then following the steps for one receiving Softly Specific feedback said, "Yes. I can totally understand why you would feel disrespected when I make those kinds of passive-aggressive comments and don't acknowledge your positive efforts. I'm sorry and apologize. In the future I'll try to not make any snarky comments and just talk to you directly and respectfully about any unhappiness."

"Thank you," George said.

Nola waited a minute to not sound defensive then said, "Now, can I share something with you using the Softly Specific?" George took a bite of her burger and nodded as she handed Nola the book with the steps of what to say in it.

"I know how this goes," Nola said. "You don't think my dad made my brother and I do this when we were in high school constantly fighting?"

"Good point," George said as she closed the book and set it next to her.

"I've let some feelings build up. I feel disappointed when you assume that doing one thing is all that's needed to remedy our whole situation. Would you please instead ask more questions like what else could I do? Do you need help preparing for the baby? Do you need me to call and make the doctor's appointment? Could you do this for me from now on?"

George nodded then said, "Yes. I can appreciate why you would feel disappointed when I don't ask more questions for how to help you out. I apologize and I'm sorry. I'll try to do that in the future."

"Thank you," Nola replied genuinely.

George waited a couple minutes then said, "I think I just assumed that because you were so mad about the fact that I was the one who landed us here in Minnesota that I've personally had to get us out of the financial mess."

"It's not all on you. I'm going to help once I can," Nola said. "But really it's more than that. I know I asked you to get a job, but when I think about it it's not just a paycheck I need. It's you stepping up and helping me prepare for the baby. I know you're at every doctor's appointment, but where are you when I'm up late at night researching car seats or reading about how to sleep train a newborn. There's so much more to kids than money."

"I always knew that but I just didn't know you wanted me to be a part of it. You were the one who wanted to carry the baby."

"That doesn't mean I'm the one who wanted to do all the work. We're in this together," Nola said.

"For richer or poorer," George added.

"You know we never actually said that in the vows we wrote," Nola pointed out.

"Doesn't matter," George said. "I've got your back. You know what sounds fun for later?"

"What?" Nola asked.

"Reading baby books," George said.

"That does sound nice," Nola replied as she took the final bite of her burger and licked her lips. It made her happy to know that George was willing to try and help with the preparation for the baby. "We probably should've gotten another one of these," she said as she crumpled up her empty wrapper.

"You want this last bite?" George asked holding up the remains of her own burger.

Nola smiled and leaned over to finish George's ButterBurger. She felt like George had heard her and George felt like Nola had heard her. Together they would have to continue to coach each other on what they needed but they were on the right path. With that thought in mind, Nola lovingly wrapped her leg around George's underneath the table in an affectionate caress.

Chapter 7

Podcast #7
Graciously Accepting Feedback
and Ownership

"Even after learning how to deliver feedback to a partner in a non-aggressive way, it is also important to learn how to genuinely receive feedback. Defensiveness escalates conflict further, yet it's one of the biggest problems I see with couples—they simply don't know how to sincerely take ownership. This leaves one's partner not feeling heard or understood, the result being no resolution.

How well do you and your partner listen, refrain from defensiveness, and sincerely apologize? If you're like most of us, you probably are not very good at this.

Without learning how to graciously and non-defensively listen to your partner's feelings and show empathetic caring it will be difficult, if not impossible, to resolve issues without residual negative feelings later resurfacing.

You must learn this skill when using the Softly Specific to resolve conflict!"

Dr. Riley sat in his chair across from the Greers. Their seventh session together had started off smoothly. They were pleased with the progress they'd made and were even laughing about how they'd been learning to co-

coach one another. It had felt a bit robotic at first, but they'd started to get the hang of using the six steps of the Softly Specific.[1] However, about twenty minutes into their session together, Daniel had brought up the fact that he didn't feel appreciated and an argument quickly resurfaced.

"I feel like she discredits everything I do at work. She acts like none of it matters if I don't help around the house," Daniel said.

"That's not true. I know he works hard. The problem is, he's always using work as an excuse. *I can't put the kids to bed, I have to send this email,* he'll say. *I can't do the dishes tonight, I've got to research this design. I can't go out to dinner on Friday, I might have to work late,*" Heather said.

"It's not an excuse. I have to work. And I don't see the problem in working," Daniel said.

"The problem is you make it a priority over our family and helping with responsibilities around the house way too often," Heather replied.

"It's not like you don't prioritize work too," Daniel said defensively.

"Yes, when I'm at work. And if I have a meeting scheduled for late in the afternoon and I know that it's going to last into dinner time, I make plans to make sure everyone is fed. I don't understand why I have to do all the work around the house, plus my own job. Why does his job take precedence over mine?"

"Because my job pays most of the bills. And the kids' education. And our vacations," he firmly stated.

"I'd happily go back to work full-time if you want. And you can be in charge of the whole household," Heather replied.

Daniel sighed and crossed his arms over his chest. It was clear they had come to this standstill before. "What are we supposed to do here?" Daniel asked. He was becoming more and more frustrated. "Everything was good last week when we were in here. And now it seems like we're fighting about the same thing again. Our jobs and work around the house."

"Yeah," Heather started. "I worry that your steps are just a technique that works fine when we're here with you. But what about in the real world? What about when things get heated? What about our deeper issues?"

---

[1] For readers interested in personally learning more detail about these six steps of the Softly Specific see *Relationship Co-Coaching: A New Approach To Deeper Love, Less Conflict* by the author.

"Deeper issues like this absolutely require that you use the Softly Specific to resolve them. Just look at what happened over the last several minutes as you both failed to use the Softly Specific. Your whole communication deteriorated into broad negative generalizations and aggressive tones. It broke down completely and resulted in each of you being defensive. You've both just been arguing back and forth," Dr. Riley said.

Heather and Daniel sighed. They knew Dr. Riley was correct and they could see where they had gone wrong. Heather recognized now that she'd complained about Daniel in a generalized way with an accusatory tone and as could be expected Daniel had reacted in a defensive way.

"Now I'm embarrassed," Heather said. "I can see why he got defensive and why this turned into an argument that went nowhere."

"Don't be embarrassed," Dr. Riley started. "Believe me, this is what happens to most everyone when they start to discuss a heated issue. You're not alone. The psychological conditioning of generalized expression of frustration with accusatory, blaming tones and defensive reactions is so deeply ingrained in our society it's hard not to act in this way. We've all been subconsciously programmed with the same ineffectual ways of dealing with conflict. It's rare to find someone who hasn't been conditioned this way. We watch people in our family life, business, and politics use these same terrible ways of trying to resolve differences and conflict and we hardly ever see someone show sincere, genuine empathy or ownership."

Heather smiled at Dr. Riley. She knew coming to see him was the right choice for her marriage but when he took the time to delve deep into their issues and explain it to them in a way that they could really understand she felt grateful to be seated on the couch in front of him. "So, what you're saying is there's hope for us?" Daniel asked.

"Of course," Dr. Riley said. "In the first 25 years that I practiced couples' therapy before developing Relationship Co–coaching, I saw that it was extraordinarily difficult for couples to break out of these kinds of recurring patterns of conflict. As a therapist, I found that the usual methods of conflict resolution and communication really didn't seem to stick or help couples break out of these patterns of conflict. So, I sat down and did some deep thinking about the nature of conflict. Then it came to me suddenly, there are really only two causes for all conflict: (1) aggressive voice tone or words and (2.) negative generalization. One or both of these two factors are present in all conflict. Think about it, have either of you ever had a conflict where one or both of these were not present?"

Daniel and Heather thought for a moment separately then looked at each other to confirm their answers. "No," they said in unison.

"Exactly," Dr. Riley said. "When either one of these two factors occur, there is an immediate defensive response in the person that you're talking to. It's like there's a deeply embedded "fight or flight" response to anything that appears to be a psychological threat to one's sense of self or esteem. A blaming or complaining tone has an implication about one's value or self-worth. This sense of perceived inner attack causes an immediate defensiveness response. Similarly, if a negative generalization is made the same defensive response will occur because the generalization is seen as completely unfair and over exaggerated."

Heather and Daniel both nodded. Dr. Riley's explanation rang true for both of them.

"The Softly Specific method for resolving conflict eliminates these two factors by being *Soft* instead of aggressive in tone and or words and by being *Specific* rather than making generalizations. To eliminate these two things you have to learn two important communication skills: (1.) share the vulnerable feelings in a respectful rather than aggressive tone and (2.) describe the specific negative behavior your partner is engaging in, rather than making any generalizations. Forget to follow these steps and it will be virtually impossible not to revert to a back-and-forth conflict."

"That all makes complete sense," Heather said. "I understand now."

"In regards to your feeling that we need to get to "deeper issues" I hear you, and to that I'd say deeper issues can't be resolved until you change the way you communicate." Dr. Riley elaborated further, "It's not about who's right or wrong in a disagreement, rather it's about how you both respectfully communicate differences and resolve them."

"We always start off respectful," Heather said.

"And then the conversation deteriorates," Daniel added. "We both feel like the other's at fault and we keep getting mad at each other."

"The only way to stop this blaming pattern is for you to both make a no-excuse agreement for any verbally aggressive behavior. You can't blame each other. So, Heather, you can't say, I wouldn't be upset if he just did more work around the house or if he just made our family more of a priority. You have to really state what's wrong and stop blaming him. Same goes for you Daniel. You both have to take responsibility."

Daniel and Heather looked at each other but neither said a word.

"Look, to move forward you're going to have to soften the way you speak to one another."

"Okay," Daniel said. "How?"

"Well, first, you know that Heather's upset about your prioritizing work too often over family, its responsibilities, and time together. So, to move forward why don't you clarify and paraphrase what she said," Dr. Riley coached Daniel.

Daniel took a deep breath then turned to Heather.

"Heather, I hear that you're frustrated that I've been working so much and not helping around the house as much as I used to."

Dr. Riley looked to Heather to confirm that's what she was upset over. Heather nodded.

"Great, now Daniel, it's your turn to show empathy to Heather's situation."

Daniel thought for a moment then began, "I can see how my prioritizing work too often over family can be upsetting and make you feel like you have to do everything on your own."

"Now, you need to apologize," Dr. Riley said.

"I'm sorry. I don't want you to feel like you're on your own. I want you to feel like we're a team," Daniel said as he reached out and placed his hand on Heather's thigh.

"Me too," Heather said as she felt the resentment flow out of her body. She finally felt heard and understood and squeezed Daniel's hand. "I want to support you too."

Dr. Riley smiled, though he knew that this was one of the lessons couples struggled with the most, he also knew it was the most important as it changed the way couples communicated for the long haul. When couples learned to co-coach in a Softly Specific manner and accept feedback and take ownership of their faults, they became stronger and lived with less conflict.

"Do you feel better now?" Dr. Riley asked.

Heather and Daniel nodded in agreement. They both knew that if they could take the blame out of their complaints and learn to apologize in an authentic sincere way without any excuses, they could get back to how they used to be—happy and a little more carefree.

~~~

After his session that day, Dr. Steve had planned on working at the home office so he and Kulap could spend time together, but when he pulled into the driveway a horn honked in the distance. *Beep. Beep.* Something was going on down by the water. *Beep.* The little beep was followed by a longer *honk* which caught Dr. Steve's attention. He made his way to the side of the house and looked out to the dock to find Chet waving from a brand-new boat.

"Come on down, Doc," Chet yelled up to Dr. Steve.

Dr. Steve walked the length of the yard straight to the dock.

"When did you get this?" he asked as he took in the shiny speedboat.

"Turns out there's a plus side to having your lady break up with you," Chet said. "Extra cash to buy the things you always wanted. Do you like it?"

"It's really nice, Chet," Dr. Steve said.

"Feel like taking it for a spin?" Chet asked as he revved the engine. The water at the back of the boat sprayed into the air gently misting Dr. Steve.

Dr. Steve looked back at the house. He'd promised Kulap that he was going to work for an hour and then he'd make time for her. He really needed to work on his podcast but a ride on the open water sounded nice.

"I'm in," Dr. Steve said then made his way onto the boat.

"There's a cooler back there," Chet said. "Grab a cold one."

Dr. Steve grabbed a beer as Chet peeled away from the dock. There was a light breeze in the air and the sun was beginning to reach that golden hour before it began to set. Chet hit the gas and the guys took off towards the other side of the lake. After ten minutes of riding at full speed, Chet slowed down and pulled into a little forested cove. There he dropped anchor.

"It's quiet out here," Dr. Steve said. "I can see why you got a boat."

"Yeah, and if she ever comes back, it'll be the perfect escape when we have a fight," Chet said.

"Or you could talk through your problems," Dr. Steve suggested.

"You still on the clock?" Chet asked. "Because I was hoping we could have some good old guy time."

"You're right," Dr. Steve said. "I guess I've been in constant work mode. With my regular clients, the podcast, a second book, and the kids and their spouses, kind of feels like I can't turn it off these days."

"How's that going?" Chet asked.

"What part?" Dr. Steve asked.

"The kids and their spouses living with you part."

"Not bad," Dr. Steve said. "It's nice having them around. And it'll be nice when Nola has the baby to have my first grandkid so close."

"So, it's not great," Chet said.

"I didn't say that," Dr. Steve said.

"You didn't have to," Chet replied. Dr. Steve gave him a look. "Come on. I know that face. That's the 'I'm trying to be nice, but I definitely have some shit on my chest that I need to unload' face."

"It's a tricky situation," Dr. Steve said. "Kulap's always been great when we've visited the kids or had them back for the holidays, but she never had children. She's not used to navigating a house full of people."

"Ah, so the love life is affected," Chet said.

"Not completely. We get along great. And I can see she's really trying with Nola and Kevin," Dr. Steve said.

"But you're not having sex," Chet added.

"You just get right to the point, don't you?" Dr. Steve replied. "And we're good in that department. We've just never been parents together. Emily and I had a system and it worked."

"I see," Chet nodded. "That must be difficult."

"It's different. If she were around, she'd know what to do with Nola and George. I mean, I know how to coach them in their relationship, but I don't know how to help her be a mom."

"Is it that different than being a dad?"

Dr. Steve looked at Chet quizzically then thought for a moment. Maybe there wasn't a difference. Maybe he could help Nola more than he thought. "You know, it's probably not. I mean obviously there's the whole breastfeeding thing, but being a parent is being a parent."

"I think you're absolutely right," Chet added. "And you probably know a whole lot more about what it takes to be a good mom from having watched Emily in the way she related to the kids and expressed her love."

Surprised and impressed Dr. Steve said, "Wow, Chet that's one of the most sensitive, enlightened things I've ever heard you say."

To this Chet quipped, "Well even a blind squirrel gets an acorn now and then." Not stopping there, he added, "Or maybe you're just seeing for the first time who the real relationship Guru is here!"

That got a good laugh from both men. Dr. Steve pondered all this further and noted, "They may be grown and married but being their dad never goes away. I know they don't want me to be too pushy and tell them exactly what to do, but I can continue to help them and their spouses with a little advice at times. They've appreciated it in the past. I just need to be careful in not stepping over the line."

"Where does Kulap fit in with all this?" Chet asked after a long a sip of his drink.

"I don't see why we can't work as a team. This could help her feel even more comfortable in fitting in with the family," Dr. Steve replied. "It might be a good reminder for us both to remember all of the things we have done well with our relationship. In particular, we've worked on our own defensiveness when it comes to arguments so maybe we can serve at times as a good example for the kids."

Chet perked up. "Oh, I saw you on Instagram the other day. You guys were amazing together," he said.

"You saw that?" Dr. Steve was surprised.

"Yeah, great advice. Not that I've ever taken it, hence this boat, but it all made sense."

"It does now, doesn't it?" Dr. Steve said as he stared out at the sun melting over the trees.

"Are we still talking about me or are we back on you?"

"I got to go home," Dr. Steve said. "There's a lot to do now. You ready?"

"Ah, sure," Chet said. "I can take you back."

Chet poured out the rest of his beer then put the can in a trash bag. He sped back to the Riley house as Dr. Steve looked out at the horizon, clearly in his own world now thinking of how he was going to talk with Kulap about how they could work together as a team in helping the kids through life.

Back at the dock Dr. Steve thanked Chet for the ride then raced up to the house. He found Kulap and asked her to join him in his office.

"Oh, are we having private time?" Kulap asked as she settled into the lounge chair across from his desk.

"Yes," Dr. Steve said. "But it's for the kids."

"The kids?" Kulap asked then smiled. "Oh good. I was wondering when we were going to talk about this whole situation. You know I like having them around, but this isn't exactly what I planned for when I retired."

"I know it's not," Dr. Steve said. "And I understand how hard that must be for you."

"I mean, it's fine and all. But they're adults living at home. When I married you, you were this successful marriage doctor with grown successful kids. Now, what are you?"

Dr. Steve sighed. "That's what I want to talk to you about."

"How to kick the kids out?"

"No," Dr. Steve said. "How to help them."

"You want my help?" Kulap asked with a surprised look. Dr. Steve had never asked for her help with the kids before. As far as their relationship was concerned the kids were part of the package of course, but they were adults who weren't going to need her. In Kulap's mind, she had no responsibility for them.

"Not only do I want your help, I need it," Dr Steve said. Kulap looked shocked. "This is all new to me too. Obviously, having the kids live here was neither of our plans. But they're here and maybe this is an opportunity for us to grow together."

"How do you mean?" Kulap asked.

"Well, I think that we could really make a difference. Remember how great it felt to work on getting everything together to buy this house. We had a mutual goal and it brought us closer."

"Yes," Kulap said as she remembered all the effort it took to sell their old place and get the financing secure for this one. "So, I have cart blanche to punish them if they disobey?" Kulap asked.

"They're not five," Dr. Steve replied. "But you have my permission to co-coach them into learning how to live on their own again."

"Oh good. I've been wanting to talk to Kevin about his future plans. Is he really going to open up a dinner theatre?"

"He might. And if he does, I need you to be supportive," Dr. Steve said.

"Okay," Kulap said. "I can do that."

"Thank you," Dr. Steve said, and he sincerely meant it. "I truly do need your help with the kids, and I want you to feel empowered as part of the family."

Kulap softened. "Wow. You've never said that before," she said.

"I mean it," Dr. Steve said as he walked over and kissed her on the forehead. He really did need Kulap's help in dealing with this new world with the kids.

~~~

Meanwhile, after a long day at school, Pilar found Kevin waiting at the car in the parking lot. Kevin was glaring at his watch, tapping his foot. Pilar approached him. Before she could even say hi, Kevin started in on her.

"You know what time it is?" he asked.

"I don't," Pilar said. "But seeing how you're staring at the clock I'm sure you do. What time is it Kevin?"

"It's exactly one hour after you said you'd meet me here," Kevin said.

"Our study group ran late, and I didn't want to miss out on the discussion," Pilar said.

"So, you left me hanging? You could've texted," Kevin said.

"I didn't want to be rude," Pilar replied.

"But making me wait isn't rude?" Kevin asked. "You know we only have one car and I wasn't going to drive all the way home to turn back around twenty minutes later and come get you."

"Well, I'm sorry to inconvenience you," she said. "You know, you wouldn't have to wait for me, if we'd just moved into campus housing like I wanted," Pilar said. "I could've walked home."

"And then what? Had dinner because I would've spent the afternoon cleaning and cooking? That sounds like a life I'd really like to have," Kevin said with a raised voice.

"Do you hear what you're saying right now? Are you trying to make some sort of sarcastic feminist point?"

"No," Kevin said. "I'm trying to tell you that this isn't exactly what I'd hoped for when we moved to Minnesota for you."

"Oh, so now it's my fault," Pilar said. "Because I don't remember you doing anything more than waiting tables back in D.C."

"Now I see how you really feel," Kevin said as he opened the driver's side door and slid inside and turned away from her.

"That's it. No more discussion?" Pilar asked as she joined him inside the car.

"I don't want to hear any more if you're going to be rude," Kevin said as he started the engine.

"You're the one who started this whole thing," Pilar replied.

"I wasn't the one who was late," Kevin said then peeled out of the parking lot.

"And because of that you're going to drive like a madman?" Pilar asked as she braced herself.

"I'm going to continue to drive how I want. In silence," Kevin said then focused on the road ahead.

They drove the entire way back to the house without a word. When they arrived, Pilar stormed out of the car and up the driveway. Kevin followed close behind and she nearly slammed the front door in his face. Kevin traipsed in as she headed straight for their room downstairs. Dr. Steve who was sitting in the family room reading a book saw the whole thing happen.

He watched as Kevin hung his head low then spoke up, "Hey, Kevin, want to join me for a second?"

"You willing to open that scotch I saw in your bar?"

"Sure," Dr. Steve said as he got up and poured two high ball glasses full of the peaty drink.

"Rough day?" Dr. Steve asked as he settled into his leather lounge chair across from Kevin who was sitting in Kulap's chair.

"The day was great. The night? Not so much," Kevin said. "My theater class has been amazing, but everything with Pilar is awful. She was an hour late tonight and as I sat and waited, I started to get mad at the fact that we were doing all of this for her. I miss our old life."

"Did you guys talk about that?"

"No. She blew up when I said I was tired of waiting. Then she said I wouldn't have to wait if I'd allowed us to move into campus housing like she'd wanted."

"So, you both blew up at each other?"

"She started it," Kevin said as he took a sip of his drink.

"Did she though?" Dr. Steve asked.

Kevin paused for a moment then admitted, "Okay. I did take a passive aggressive tone with her when I pointed out she was late."

"And you know what that does," Dr. Steve said.

"Yes, dad. I know all the steps to being Softly Specific. I know we're not supposed to be aggressive with one another when we talk. But sometimes that's just how I feel."

"And how do you feel now?" Dr. Steve asked.

"Not great," Kevin admitted.

"So, do you think you two need to work on recommitting to using the Softly Specific?"

"I mean, we made a pact that there would never be an excuse for becoming verbally aggressive like you talked about in your podcast but that's always easier said than done. I don't know how your clients do it."

"Well, they definitely don't do it over night," Dr. Steve replied. "Even Kulap and I have our moments. When we do, we pause and remember how to talk to one another."

"I don't think there was any space for us to pause tonight," Kevin said.

"Is that really true? Could you have calmly stated that you felt disrespected that Pilar was late?"

"Sure," Kevin started. "But I was also mad. I'm still kind of mad. When I first told her that I was going to take that theater class she was excited for me and it felt like we were both going to support each other in following our dreams here. Yet, I've been taking classes for almost a month now and except for that first day she hasn't asked me one question about my day to day."

"Have you told her this?"

"No. That would be too easy," Kevin smiled as he finished his scotch.

"So, you think you need to talk to her?"

"Of course," Kevin said. "But I also needed to vent to my old man too."

"You can do that any time," Dr. Steve said.

"Thanks, Dad. And thanks for the drink. I'm gonna go talk to my wife now."

"Great idea," Dr. Steve said and watched happily as Kevin walked off. It felt good to be able to help his son with his marriage. After all, what good was all of his work with his clients if he couldn't help his own family.

~~~

When Kevin got to their room, he found Pilar in bed, covers pulled up to her neck. Kevin sat at the edge of the mattress and waited for her to notice. Pilar didn't say a word. Kevin took that as a sign that he needed to be the one to initiate conversation.

"That's not how I wanted our day to end," Kevin said.

"Me either," Pilar said as she pulled the covers off and sat up in bed.

"I jumped at you," Kevin said. "I shouldn't have done that."

"Yes. But I shouldn't have taken you for granted. I know you have a life and dreams too. I've just been overwhelmed with school and that's not an excuse, but I've definitely used it as a way to justify neglecting us."

"I want you to succeed. I know that you're going to do amazing things with this degree. I just don't want us to forget who we are as a couple. This was a lot easier in D.C.," Kevin sighed.

"When we both had our own priorities," Pilar added.

"Exactly," Kevin said.

"I'm sorry I said that all you did was wait tables. I know that you've been doing far more than that. I know you have a business plan for your theater. And I can understand how my comment about you just being a waiter was offensive. There's no excuse for it. I knew what I was saying."

"Thank you," Kevin said. "That means a lot."

Kevin sat down next to Pilar on the bed.

"I'm not used to having to rely on someone for rides. I miss the subway," she said.

"Me too," Kevin said. "But this is what we've got for now."

"We could move closer to school," Pilar said softly.

"How?" Kevin asked. He was intrigued. As much as he liked saving money by living at his dad's house, he also liked the idea of each of them having their independence again.

"There's a guy in my class, Trevor. He rented an entire house by campus and has an extra room he's trying to rent out," Pilar said.

"Hmmm," Kevin said. "Does he know you have a husband?"

"Of course. What kind of question is that?" Pilar asked.

"I don't know. Just making sure that he knew he'd be renting to us and not just you."

"So, you'll consider it?"

"I'm willing to take a look," Kevin said. "But no guarantees. We do have a free place to stay right now and it's nice not to pay rent. Plus, when my business takes off, I'll need some starting capital."

"That's true," Pilar said. "So, it's a maybe?"

Kevin nodded. "Can we also agree not to be aggressive and to express our softer vulnerable feelings? And to especially show more empathy and ownership right off the bat with one another to avoid these kinds of fights."

"Sure," Pilar said. "You sound like your dad."

Kevin smiled. "I do, don't I? But he's right. I think it would really help to follow exactly what he says in his book and what we've been hearing in his podcasts about resolving conflict with the Softly Specific. We've been talking about doing it more often, but you can see what happens when we don't. Let's make a pact to try and always do this."

"Done," Pilar replied. She liked seeing this more assertive version of Kevin. "Are you coming to bed now?"

Kevin smiled and climbed under the covers. They snuggled for a moment, then Pilar got antsy.

"Want to see what I did?" Pilar said as she turned and grabbed a notebook off her nightstand. She opened it to a page where there was a chart and arrows with names of different celebrities, prominent figures and a few athletes. "I call it six degrees of baby bacon."

Kevin stared at her creation in awe. "Oh, I get it. Like six degrees of Kevin Bacon."

"Yeah. I figured Kevin Bacon would be too obvious a choice as the baby's father but I figured there'd be a link if we start with him."

"You're really determined to find this out, aren't you?" Kevin asked.

"Aren't you the least bit curious?" Pilar asked.

"I mean it would be cool to be related to Harrison Ford," Kevin replied.

"He's far too old," Pilar said as she shook her head.

"He's Indiana Jones. He's got stamina," Kevin replied.

"You do have a point," Pilar laughed as she fell into Kevin's arms.

He held her tight as they looked through the notebook of possibilities. It felt good to talk through their problems in a kind non-defensive way and create a plan for how to better handle their conflicts in the future.

Kevin was glad they'd talked through their issue. He could've let the problem fester and they could've ignored it and gone about the rest of their week pretending they hadn't blown up at each other. But he knew that that would only lead to resentment down the road. He was happy he'd talked to his dad and taken initiative to make things right with Pilar.

He turned on his side and looked affectionately into Pilar's eyes, then said sweetly, "Good night, my little Sherlock Holmes. Maybe tomorrow we'll crack the case."

He kissed her and curled up against her. She responded in kind as her body gently melded, cuddling into his. That night he and Pilar slept soundly in each other's arms with no worries, only feelings of renewed hopefulness about their future.

Chapter 8

Podcast #8
A New Concept of Love for the 21st Century:
Altruistic Love
and Relationship Self–Actualization

"Most people have great difficulty in making real change in their relationship. They lack a stronger desire to really understand and go out of their way to meet the needs of their partner. The problem is that culturally transmitted concepts about relationships and marriage promote self-centered expectations about romantic love.

This me-focused type of love pushes couples farther away from the simple solution to most of their relationship problems—unselfishly meeting one another's love needs!

What is suggested here is a radical change in thinking to a new concept of Relationship Self-Actualization based on altruistic, unselfish love. All of us take full responsibility when entering any relationship for doing everything possible to meet the most significant emotional love needs of our partner. That's a very different way of looking at romantic love and marriage, isn't it?"

"Is this what's missing?" Heather asked Daniel as she turned down the volume on Dr. Riley's podcast. They were on their way to their next appointment with the doctor and were catching up on the latest episode of his "Relationship Co-Coaching."

Daniel nodded. "I know I've definitely been a little selfish when it comes to our relationship."

"Me too," Heather said in agreement.

"I'm hoping he tells us it's not our fault again," Daniel replied with a laugh.

"You heard what he said," Heather started then quoted Dr. Riley, "It's human nature to be relatively self-centered, especially in a me-oriented society."

"That's definitely been me," Daniel said. "I feel terrible."

"Don't feel bad," Heather said. "It's not like my life goals have been around being the best wife."

"You're a great wife," Daniel said.

"Thank you," Heather replied. "But you know what I mean. Have we really been unselfishly trying to meet one another's needs?"

Daniel shook his head no as he pulled into the parking lot of Dr. Riley's. "Good thing we've been doing these sessions."

"Seriously," Heather smiled. She was glad that Daniel was on the same page as her and was committed to their appointments with Dr. Riley. Maybe they hadn't figured everything out with their relationship yet, but at least they were putting in the effort and working on it together.

Upstairs, Dr. Riley greeted them with the same friendly smile he'd been giving them over the last two months.

"Welcome back," he said. "How was the week?"

"Great," Daniel said. "But we're ready to jump right in and learn about altruistic love and relationship self-actualization."

Dr. Riley looked surprised at the use of his own terminology.

"We were listening to you on the way over here," Heather explained. "We've got questions."

"Then I've got answers," Dr. Riley said as he settled into his chair and pulled out his notepad. "So, tell me what's going on?"

"Well, we both acknowledge that we haven't made our relationship a priority," Heather started.

"It's almost like we took the relationship for granted and figured we'd just work on a few details and it'd all be good," Daniel said.

"I understand," Dr. Riley began. "Many couples have the same problem. There's an underlying belief system in our society that dominates our cultural thinking. We place focus on occupational and economic achievement in life, but there's no priority placed on setting a life goal for achievement in a relationship."

"That's exactly what we realized," Daniel said. "I love Heather. I want to keep working on listening non-defensively and meeting her love needs. I want us to keep co-coaching each other but clearly there's more to do, right?"

Dr. Riley nodded. "Working on all of these things is imperative, but if there isn't that bigger commitment to prioritize your relationship and find value in reaching that achievement of loving unselfishly, you'll fall back into old patterns."

"I definitely don't want that," Heather said as she noted how much their relationship had improved over the last few sessions. "I feel like we're actually communicating now. I want to keep this going."

"I do too," Daniel said. "So, what do we do, doctor? Simply say I commit to loving you unselfishly?"

Dr. Riley shook his head. "Is that what you do when you want a raise or a promotion? Do you just say I'm committing to a raise and hope it happens?"

"No. If I want something at work, I have to come up with a plan to reach my goal," Daniel said confidently. "And once I have that plan, I have to work towards it daily. My goal is always at the back of my mind so that every move I make is leading towards it."

"It's the same thing with marriage," Dr. Riley replied. "Most every action either moves you toward self-actualization and altruistic love or away from it."

"That makes sense to me," Daniel replied. "This isn't something you sit back and say, oh I love you, and that's enough."

"Exactly," Dr. Riley said. "How do you feel, Heather?"

"I guess for me, it's not that I never had marriage goals, but it's that I always held back when I didn't feel the same from him. I guess it was a little bit of tit for tat, right? Like, if he's going to focus on work then why would I spend all this time focusing on our marriage?"

"I can understand that," Dr. Riley said. "Achievement of marital happiness is not given the same priority as work-related material success and so it probably felt like you were wishing for something that didn't really contribute to the big picture of your life. But let me assure you it does."

"So, what are the steps we need to take to do this?" Daniel, ever the doer, asked.

"You've already taken the first step," Dr. Riley began, "Admitting that attaining the highest level of achievement in your romantic relationship is not at the same level of priority as your job and financial goals is how you start."

"Okay, I can admit that," Daniel said.

Heather nodded. She was on board too. "What else? Do what I can to make him happy?" she asked.

"Yes and no. Yes, your purpose should be to truly make Daniel happy. But this isn't a self-denying approach; rather it's a mutually altruistic relationship in which both partners seek to meet the important love needs of one another. It's not about giving in to your partner with a feeling that you were the one who had to compromise; rather it's giving to her or him unselfishly. This attitude will help tremendously in reducing conflict in your relationship."

"Okay," Heather said. "I can do that. Daniel?"

Daniel nodded. "I can do it too," he said.

"And remember," Dr. Riley said. "It's like anything else: If you don't have a goal, then you won't likely be successful in achieving it. Make relationship self-actualization and unselfish love a driving achievement goal in your life, and then you're bound to be successful."

"I'm setting that goal right now," Daniel said.

"And you know what that means?" Dr. Riley asked.

"The same thing it does when I'm working towards a raise," Daniel said. "I think about it every day and I plan how every action I take or don't take works to reach my goal."

"Exactly," Dr. Riley said. "Watch yourself, monitor the NRPs you've committed to change, and ask for frequent feedback whenever you might fall off-track. Most importantly, go out of your way to meet the unique emotional love needs of Heather at every opportunity. Sometimes couples will ask what is the "technique" to achieving this relationship self-actualization. I tell them it's about placing your romantic relationship at the highest level of priority in life. That level should be equal to or higher than your occupational and material achievement. And to really make it a priority, you'll need to pull out that list of written love needs and periodically review it. Ask yourself and ask Heather how well you are doing in fulfilling those needs for one another. This may seem mechanical, but there is no other way to make sure that in the busyness of life you don't forget, slip back into old patterns, and become complacent. This is the best way to really inject that kind of deep, passionate unselfish love into your relationship. It will bring the deepest, most profound kind of love and connectedness a couple can experience in a truly self-actualized relationship," Dr. Riley finished.

"And that's exactly what we're going to do from here on out," Heather said as she looked lovingly at Daniel.

~~~

The sun had begun to set over Humble Lake when Dr. Steve arrived home. On his way into the house, he passed Kevin and Pilar who were headed out.

"Where are you two off to?" Dr. Steve asked.

"Dinner," Pilar said. "I cancelled my study group tonight. Kevin's taking me on a date."

Kevin smiled. He'd been wanting to do something special for Pilar for a while now but they'd both been too busy with school. He had declared tonight date night so that they could spend some good quality time together.

"Enjoy," Dr. Steve said as the two walked off to their car.

"Thanks, Dad," Kevin called back as he opened the passenger side door for Pilar.

Dr. Steve smiled at the sight. Kevin and Pilar's relationship had been growing stronger over the last week and he liked to think that his talk with his son had something to do with it. Small gestures like opening the car door, archaic or not, showed that Kevin was committed to putting Pilar first, which Kevin knew helped her feel truly loved. Pilar's prioritizing their relationship for an evening instead of her degree showed that Pilar had made the same commitment. Dr. Steve happily watched them drive off then headed inside.

Upon walking into the house, Dr. Steve was overwhelmed with the most delicious smell. The scent of garlic and butter mixed with a little wine wafted through the air. He took a deep breath and wondered, was Kulap making him a date night surprise? But when he made his way to the kitchen, he found George and Nola donned in aprons, laughing as they flitted about the kitchen, adding a dash of this and a dab of that.

"Well, look at you two," Dr. Steve said. "This looks lovely. Should Kulap and I make plans to go out so you can have a night to yourself?"

"No way," George began. "This is for you guys. There was a deal at the store on shrimp and with my employee discount it was like it was free."

"We wanted to do something nice for you guys for letting us stay here," Nola added.

"Isn't this lovely?" Kulap said as she entered the room holding a glass of white wine.

"Really nice," Dr. Steve said as he took a sip of Kulap's wine. "Is there more of this?"

"Of course," George said as she poured Dr. Steve a glass of his own.

"Dinner's almost ready," Nola said as she turned down the burner on the stove. "Everyone, take a seat."

George helped Nola plate the dinners and bring them to the table. The four of them sat around and enjoyed their meals as they talked about their days.

"Should we tell them?" George asked Nola.

"Yes," Nola said.

"I knew there was a reason for this dinner," Kulap said.

"It's a good reason," Nola said with a smile.

"We've been discussing our birthing plan and we want you two to be there," George said.

"Not like, there, there, because that just feels too weird, but we want you to be the first of our family to meet the little one," Nola said.

Dr. Steve put down his fork and smiled. "We would be honored," he said.

Kulap, never one to miss a beat and always on top of all the logistics asked, "Is the father coming?"

"Maybe," Nola said.

"So, we'll get to know his identity before everyone else?" Kulap said excitedly.

"Maybe?" George asked with a surprised tone as she ignored Kulap. This was all news to her.

"I don't know, it's just something I've been thinking about. We can discuss it later," Nola replied trying to brush George off. She wanted dinner to be about the fun parts of the future—her dad holding his grandbaby for the first time, not about their relationship squabbles.

"I thought we had discussed it," George said. From the beginning the plan had always been that George and Nola would be the primary parents. The sperm donor would be like a fun uncle, but he wouldn't have a say in how the baby was raised.

"We did," Nola replied. She hesitated to say more, but she couldn't say nothing. "I've been thinking that it might be nice to have a male presence around."

Kulap sensed the tension and nudged Dr. Steve under the table.

"You know," Dr. Steve started. "I'm happy to take over that role as grandpa."

"I know, dad," Nola began. "And I'm one hundred percent positive that you're going to be the best Papa ever, but I was thinking… What happens when the baby gets older and curious and starts asking questions? We're clearly his or her parents but not fully biologically. Wouldn't it be nice if all of us were involved from the beginning?"

"I can see how that would be an important consideration," Dr. Steve said.

Nola said then turned to George. "I'm not saying we have to do it my way, I'm just saying there are things we might not have considered when we started this venture."

George pushed slightly away from the table. It was a small movement, but Dr. Steve could see it was a sign that what Nola said really bothered her.

Dr. Steve knew he needed to say something to ease the situation. "If there's anything I know about parenting to be one hundred percent true and effective, it's that both parents need to be on the same page. You're going to have to work on this together," Dr. Steve said.

"True, sir, very true," George replied.

"So, we will work on it, right, George?" Nola asked. She hoped that this would quell any more discussion at the table.

"Absolutely," George replied gently. She understood that this was not the time or place to get into it further.

"But we still get to be the first ones to know who the baby's father is, right?" Kulap asked.

Dr. Steve shot her a look. "What?!" she said. "Okay, you can tell us when you want."

"*If* you want," Dr. Steve added.

~~~

After dinner, George and Nola retreated to their room. Nola went straight to the dresser and started tidying up. George was frustrated.

"Are we going to talk about this?" George asked in reference to their discussion at dinner.

"Yes," Nola said. "But first I have to finish this." Nola said as she pulled out a very organized binder with all of the research she'd been doing in preparation for the baby. There were book lists and pictures of things they still needed to purchase. Numbers of pediatricians and notes on breastfeeding.

George sighed at the sight. "I wish you put this much effort into our relationship," George said.

"You know I love you," Nola replied.

"I know," George said. "But can you see how it's a little frustrating for me. It's like you want me to have all these life goals – get a job, be financially secure—but when I want to focus on us, you kind of blow it off."

"I'm not blowing it off," Nola said. "We've been working on these things. Our NRP's, being direct about what it is we need to feel loved. I thought we were getting somewhere."

"We are," George said. "It's just that sometimes I don't feel like you're that interested in us. I feel like you're more interested in achieving things.

Having a wife that has a good job. A partner who's a good parent. A career of your own. What's so wrong about having a good marriage too?"

"Nothing. We have a good marriage," Nola said.

"Are you really committed to this?" George asked. "'Cause it kind of feels like I'm an afterthought lately."

"No you're not," Nola replied. She didn't understand where this was coming from. To her, they were fine. "Look, I'm stressed. And you know that when I'm stressed I focus on the details. I want everything to be perfect for this baby. I want him or her to have everything they want and need."

"And they will," George said. "But none of that will matter if you and I are fighting."

"We're not fighting. Are we?" Nola asked surprised that George would even say that. To her this wasn't a fight. To her it was just a talk about the things they'd observed.

"No. I guess not," George replied. But even as she said that she didn't feel like she was being one hundred percent honest. She felt like she was doing all these things to improve herself to meet Nola's love needs, but she worried that Nola wasn't reciprocating. She worried Nola wasn't as committed as she was.

That night, the two barely slept. Each was worried about their future in their own way, but neither was ready to take the discussion further. Instead, they both tossed and turned until dawn when George had to wake for her job at the grocery store.

~~~

The next morning, after George had gone to work, Nola decided to call the baby's biological father. They had been friends back on the west coast and she needed an outside opinion on everything that was happening with George. Since he was, in many ways, a part of the family she didn't see the issue with calling him.

They had been catching up for about ten minutes – doing the small talk sort of thing, when Nola finally got into the real reason she was calling.

"I'm worried," she said, "that George isn't going to be the most reliable partner."

"But you loved her carefree nature when you met her. Isn't that why you fell in love?" he asked with a deep voice.

"Of course," Nola said. "But I also wasn't bringing another life into the world then."

"So? You had your life and having George in it was a blessing. I think you used those exact words back then," he said. "Why wouldn't it be the same for the baby?"

Nola sighed. He was right. George really was a blessing to her rigid and over controlled life. Maybe she was the one overreacting to everything. Maybe she was the one who needed to change. Nola thought about this and realized that maybe she needed the help of her father. She made a mental note to talk to him before George returned from work. However, just as she had that thought and said her goodbyes to the baby's father, George walked in with her hands on her hips, clearly upset.

"How long were you standing there?" Nola asked.

"Long enough to know we need to figure this out," George replied. "I was fine last night when you said this was just a stress thing. But this isn't just about stress is it?"

Nola shook her head, "I don't know."

"What do you mean you don't know?" George asked. She was upset at the way Nola became passive in situations that really mattered to their lives. She didn't want to fight with her wife, but she also didn't want to just brush over the whole issue.

"Talking to him made me realize what I have," Nola said.

"That's great. But why couldn't you talk to me?" George asked. She was genuinely hurt by the fact that Nola hadn't come to her. "When we agreed to have this baby, we agreed that we were a family. You, me and whatever kids we had. We were supposed to figure out anything that related to the baby together. This was a mutual goal. Right?"

Nola nodded. George was saying exactly what they had talked about and agreed upon. She hung her head. She knew she was in the wrong.

"Why do you always run to someone else when things go wrong?"

"I don't do that," Nola said defensively.

"Really? Because from what I've seen that's exactly what you do. You ran to your friends when we got in little spats in LA. You ran to your dad all the way here in Minnesota when we got in financial trouble. And now you're running to our baby's father because we got in a disagreement. Why can't you talk to me?"

"I can," Nola said.

"But you don't," George replied.

"I'm here now," Nola said.

"Yes, because I came home early to surprise you. I felt bad about our talk last night and I bought this label maker because I wanted to help organize all the things we'd gotten for the baby. I was trying to make you happy. Not for any other reason but to show that I loved you."

Nola sat down on the bed. "Really?"

"Yes," George said. "I don't know why you can't see that I'm trying to make this work."

"I see it," Nola replied. "I just have a hard time accepting it. I think we might need help."

George nodded in agreement.

"I'm going to go get my dad," Nola said.

"I told you, you always run to him," George said.

"I deserved that," Nola smiled. "But I'm still getting him," she said as she left the room.

When Nola returned with Dr. Steve in tow, she sat on the bed next to George and motioned for her dad to have a seat in the glider chair Kulap had purchased for them in anticipation of Nola needing a comfortable spot to nurse the baby.

Dr. Steve took a seat then turned to them both. "Tell me what happened," he said.

"Same old fight, sir," George started.

"I just can't seem to let go of this resentment I have towards George," Nola said.

"I'm trying here," George said. "I don't feel like anything I do is good enough. She tells me what she needs to feel loved, but when I do it, it's never correct."

"Are you both committed to loving each other unselfishly?" Dr. Steve asked.

"Of course," Nola said.

"I don't think so," George said.

"Okay, first you both need to get on the same page," Dr. Steve said. "If you want to be the best parents to that baby of yours, you need to commit to a fully self-actualized relationship."

"Sir, you're going to have to back up a little bit and explain that to me," George said.

"What I mean by "self-actualization" is simply putting in the effort to achieve your highest potential in life. And I don't mean financial or career wise, I mean your highest potential as a partner in this relationship. This also means there's no back and forth. No blaming each other. You both have to commit to love unselfishly. You have to agree to come at this from the point of view that this is something you're both working towards. This is as big of a goal as getting enough money to pay off your debts and move into your own place. You need to think about it constantly and work towards that goal."

"Okay," George said taking it all in.

"We can work on achieving that," Nola added.

"And do you know how you'll know that you've arrived and achieved that goal? Well, the answer is: when both of you feel so incredibly, deeply loved from having consciously and intentionally met one another's love needs. Of course in order to get there you need to explore and find out exactly what those things are and then remember to do them for one another on a daily basis," Dr. Steve said.

"I can commit to that," George said.

"Me too," Nola replied.

"True. Little miss organized over here is good at goals," George said with a laugh.

"Are you being facetious?" Nola asked.

"No. I'm being serious. I think that between the two of us if we put our minds to it, we can make this work."

Nola softened. "You're right. We did move cross country because that was our best option and we made that work."

"Exactly," George said.

"So my question for both of you is after now making this commitment with one another, how could you resolve the conflict you just had?" Dr. Steve asked.

"Well, I have to honestly admit that I wasn't thinking about the highest priority of our relationship or George's feelings and certainly not how to unselfishly meet her love needs," Nola responded. She then turned to George. "If I had, then I never would have made the mistake of making that call without first discussing it with you. You're my partner. I can see how it's a really important love need for you. I should always talk with you first especially when it's anything regarding our child. So, I can completely understand why you would be upset, and I apologize."

"Thank you" George responded. "And I really can appreciate your fears about my reliability because of past mistakes. I am truly sorry about that. Your need to feel secure is something I'm totally dedicated to try and meet."

Dr. Steve watched as they both softened. "So, are you two good now?" he asked.

"Good as a couple where one half is a hormonal wreck can be," Nola responded.

"I love this hormonal wreck," George said. "And I love this family."

"Me too," Dr. Steve said as he stood up and wrapped his arms around both of them. He felt content that he had helped them with an important issue and commit to this new way of looking at relationships motivated by unselfish love. As they broke from their embrace, George placed one hand on Nola's belly.

"You hear that, little one," she said, "we all love you."

Dr. Steve smiled at the sight and Nola smiled at her father watching George. Together the three of them quietly enjoyed the deep wonder and awe of the newly growing bonds of their family.

Chapter 9

Podcast #9
The Four Types of Closeness in Any
Relationship

"One big problem with couples is that they have made other things in life more important than their relationship. Allowing this to happen can be a mistake. Once a couple begins to spend less time together, it's easy to grow apart and to fall back into negative feelings of hurt and resentment.

Why does this happen so often? It can happen when couples neglect one or more of the four ways to be close in a relationship.

Now, let's take a look at and explore and consider how you and your partner can become better in these four types of closeness in a relationship:

The Four Types of Closeness

1) Conversational intimacy
2) Shared interests and activities
3) Physical affection
4) Sex"

The Greens were forty-five minutes into their session with Dr. Riley and had reviewed the work they'd done so far. It was clear to all parties that they'd made great progress. Sure, they'd had moments of regression, but they were committed to the process and were ready for the next step. The next step was understanding how to become closer to one another.

"I have to say," Daniel started, "After listening to your podcast this week it finally feels like we get to move on to the fun stuff."

"It is fun, but it's important too," Dr. Riley stated.

"Of course. Obviously, this doesn't mean we're going to forget everything we learned," Heather added. "But it's been nice. We started doing this thing where we take a walk around the neighborhood after dinner and we talk, just the two of us," Heather said. "Sometimes it's only for five or ten minutes, but it's far better than we've been doing."

"Yeah. The kids do their homework and we get to connect again," Daniel said. "I love the kids, but when they're in the room, they're our only focus."

"Understandably," Dr. Riley said. "And, have these walks helped?"

"Absolutely," Heather said.

"I'll admit. I was reluctant at first, but they really have made a difference. It's crazy how much that short amount of time walking and talking makes us feel like we're a real couple again, not just parents trying to hold everything together."

"Spending time together is important to keeping it together. Once a couple begins to spend less time with one another, it's easier to fall back into negative feelings of hurt and resentment that lead to emotional distance," Dr. Riley said.

"Which is where we were before we came to see you," Daniel said. Heather nodded in agreement. They were quite distant when they began therapy, but now they were doing things together.

"You know what's crazy. We signed up to do a 5k in a month and on some of our walks we've started jogging," Heather added.

"That's great," Dr. Riley said. "Having a mutual goal creates opportunities to do more things together. It sounds like you're really working on the four types of closeness," Dr. Riley said with a smile.

"We're doing our best," Daniel replied as he gently placed his arm around Heather and gave her an affectionate squeeze. Heather melted into his chest. It was evident that they had been not only creating moments of conversational intimacy and time to work on their shared interests, but that they were also paying attention to how they demonstrated affection towards one another.

Dr. Riley smiled at the two of them and reflected back to the first day that the Greens set foot in his office. It was a completely different situation than the one in front of him now. Months ago, they sat on opposite sides of the couch. Their body language said it all. There was no sense of affection between them. It was clear that day that they had lost whatever sort of closeness they once had. Today, however, it was evident that they were once again becoming close to one another.

Heather squeezed Daniel's thigh then lifted her head from his shoulder. "Should we tell him?"

"Is it appropriate?" Daniel asked.

"Nothing is off limits here," Dr. Riley said.

"We also asked my parents to come and stay with the kids this weekend and we booked two nights away at a cabin in Door County on the lake."

"That sounds romantic," Dr. Riley said.

"That's what we're hoping," Daniel said with a smile.

"Well," Dr. Riley started, "It seems to me like you guys are doing pretty well right now."

"Thanks to you," Heather said.

"Enjoy your weekend, then," Dr. Riley replied as he got up from his chair.

"We will," Daniel replied as he helped Heather get up from the couch. Together, the two walked out of Dr. Riley's office holding hands.

~~~

Dr. Steve was driving the winding road to his house when he had an idea. After working with the Greens that day it had occurred to him that he'd been so wrapped up in sessions with his clients, the podcast, and the kids all moving home that he had neglected many of the elements he was teaching his clients in his own relationship.

While things were good between him and Kulap, he knew that if he continued down this path it would be easy for them to slip out of closeness and become more distant.

He missed moments like the one they had on their first night in their new home—sipping champagne and having a picnic on their living room floor. As he caught a glimpse of the lake from the road, he decided to call Chet and ask for a favor.

Chet agreed to help Dr. Steve. Now it was time to put his plan in motion. At the next stop sign he turned right instead of left and headed to the store where he bought a bottle of wine and a few assorted appetizers he knew Kulap loved.

Twenty minutes later, he arrived at Chet's house. Chet was at the dock taking the cover off his boat. Dr. Steve walked down the slight hill to join him. There was a bounce to his step that Chet hadn't seen in a while.

"Oh, someone's trying to get lucky tonight," Chet said as he took note of the wine and other ingredients in Dr. Steve's bag.

"This is how you keep a relationship alive," Dr. Steve said with a smile.

"It looks like something out of my old college playbook," Chet laughed. Dr. Steve gave Chet a look. "I'm kidding. Everything still going all right?"

"Just need a night to ourselves to focus on us," Dr. Steve replied. "Thanks for letting me borrow the boat. I owe you."

"Free session next week?" Chet asked. "Bree agreed to have dinner with me on Friday."

"Really?" Dr. Steve was surprised. He hadn't heard Bree's name since the day Bree left him.

Chet nodded. "I miss her. I don't want to mess it up this time."

"Good luck, just focus on her needs and you'll make her happy!" Dr. Steve said as he placed his groceries in the boat. "Anything I need to know about driving this?"

"Just a standard speedboat. Don't run it aground and you're good to go," Chet said.

"I can handle that," Dr. Steve said then started the engine. Chet released the lines holding the boat at the dock and pushed it away. "I'll have it back later," Dr. Steve promised.

"Keep it as late as you need," Chet said with a smile. Dr. Steve nodded then backed the boat out into the lake and sped off towards his home.

Before he'd arrived at Chet's, Dr. Steve sent Kulap a text message telling her to meet him at the dock at five-thirty. As he approached the house, he saw Kulap waiting at the water's edge. She was sitting on the end of the dock with her toes dangling in the water, staring off into the distance. He hadn't told her any bit of his plan and so he was sure she probably had no clue that it was him approaching in the boat.

Dr. Steve throttled back the engine and slowly approached Kulap. She looked concerned, but when she could finally make out his face, she jumped up and began waving. Dr. Steve maneuvered the boat next to the dock.

"Did you buy a boat?" Kulap asked. "We don't have the budget for that."

"Relax," Dr. Steve said. "I borrowed it from Chet."

"Thank god," Kulap said. "I couldn't take another surprise at this moment."

"The only surprise is me here waiting to take you on a date," Dr. Steve said as he reached out his hand and helped her on deck.

"This is one of the best surprises I've had in a while," Kulap said.

"Good," Dr. Steve replied as he gave her a gentle kiss. "I wanted us to have alone time. Talking like we always have. Just you and I sharing a good conversation together."

Kulap smiled then looked down at the bag of groceries. "You got my favorite—the cracked pepper water crackers."

"Anything for you," Dr. Steve said. She gave him a quick kiss then sat in the passenger seat as Dr. Steve revved the engine and they headed out to the middle of the lake. The wind whipped through their hair and they both relaxed into the moment.

"I was worried with the kids around that you'd forgotten about our promise to have these moments," Kulap said.

"It might not be as frequent as it was before, but I'd never give these up," Dr. Steve assured her.

Dr. Steve drove them to a cove on the other side of the lake where the water was calm. He dropped anchor then opened the bottle of wine and set out a plate full of Kulap's favorite crackers along with some cheeses and other appetizers. Kulap was impressed with Dr. Steve's plan.

For two hours they sat as the sun set behind them. They talked about everything from their own relationship, to their future plans, to the kids and their soon to be grandkid. Nothing was off limits and nothing was rushed. These conversations created the types of moments that brought them closer. Having time with no distractions to simply sit and talk made them both feel content in their relationship. Together they vowed to make more time to have deep talks like this.

"I could get used to nights out here on the water," Kulap said.

"Me too," Dr. Steve replied. "It might mean I'll be giving Chet free therapy for life, but it'll be well worth it," he finished as he leaned over and kissed Kulap.

~~~

A couple days later, Kulap and Dr. Steve still felt a renewed sense of connection from their conversation out on the water. They were in the kitchen making breakfast, stealing a kiss here and there. It was a Saturday and they'd both woken up early. The smell of coffee and toast wafted through the house. When Nola appeared, Dr. Steve was holding his mug to Kulap's lips so she could taste his freshly brewed South African blend.

"Awww, could you guys be any cuter?" Nola remarked at the sight.

"We're trying," Dr. Steve said.

"You really do practice what you preach, don't you?" Nola replied.

"Of course, he does," Kulap said. "That's why I married him."

"How are things with George?" Dr. Steve asked.

"Fine. Good, actually," Nola said as she grabbed a piece of toast and poured a glass of orange juice.

"Did you –" Dr. Steve started, but Nola interrupted.

"Yes, Dad. We listened to your episode this week," Nola said.

Dr. Steve smiled. "Any questions?"

Nola shook her head as she took a bite of toast. She and George had discussed all the types of closeness and had decided to work on each aspect on their own time.

"Okay, well, you know I'm here if you need anything," Dr. Steve said.

"I know," Nola replied.

"Should we eat?" Kulap asked sensing that Nola was ready to move on from the conversation.

"Yes," Nola said. "Did you make eggs?"

Dr. Steve nodded and presented Nola with a plate and they all sat down to breakfast.

~~~

Later that afternoon, Kevin and Pilar sat on the back patio across from one another lost in their phones. They were both reading the news, scrolling through social media, catching up on emails. Pilar got a notification that Dr. Steve's next podcast episode would be out on Monday which reminded her of that week's episode on closeness. She and Kevin had listened to it already but they hadn't exactly made the effort to implement any of the advice. She looked over at Kevin who was still distracted by the glowing screen in his hand and decided to remedy that fact.

"We got to get out of here," she said. "This is our one day off. If we were still in DC, we'd be out doing something fun. Exploring the city."

Kevin put down his phone and looked up at her. "You're right," he said as he thought about the fact that they used to love their weekends together at their old place. Their shared interest in checking out the newest coffee shop and browsing books at their favorite bookstore had kept their relationship exciting. But now that they were here in Minnesota, they'd gotten relaxed in their efforts to maintain that sort of closeness. They'd become too wrapped up in school and work and forgotten to put in the effort for each other.

"Want to head downtown?" Pilar suggested.

"Yes," Kevin smiled.

Forty-five minutes later just as the sun had begun to set, Pilar parked at a meter on a hip little street in downtown St. Paul. There was a brewery, a coffee shop, a record store, and at the corner—a bookstore. Down the way was a crowded little restaurant.

"This is fun," Kevin said as he took in his surroundings. The street reminded him of their neighborhood back in DC. They had spent plenty of nights heading out to dinner, then grabbing a drink, and perusing their local bookstore. They had this habit of going to the self-help section and opening up the astrology books on relationships. They would then read about how compatible they were based on their signs and how to deal with each other's quirks. Pilar always bought into it, but Kevin was much more of a skeptic. Yet, astrology had been one of the things that had connected them early on in their relationship. Despite their differing beliefs, astrology was a shared interest that always pulled them together.

After they exited the car, Pilar led them down the street past the restaurant and coffee shop and towards the bookstore.

"Should we do our thing?" Kevin asked as they approached the front door to Covered Pages bookstore.

"Yes," Pilar said with a smile. She knew exactly what he meant.

They made their way to the self-help section, grabbed a couple astrology books and settled in to a cozy couch where they started sharing what they'd read—debating the perks of her fire sign and his air sign. They both relaxed into the moment as feelings of nostalgia and closeness rose within them.

"It's nice to be doing this again," Pilar said.

"It really is," Kevin replied. He was about to lean over and kiss Pilar when she pulled away.

"Is that Anna Klup?" she whispered to Kevin and gestured over his left shoulder. Kevin slowly turned so as not to be super obvious. Then he saw the woman Pilar was looking at and gasped.

"It's her," he replied softly.

Anna Klup was famous in the puppetry circles, which meant nothing to the general population but clearly meant a lot to Kevin. Pilar knew this. "Let's follow her," she said.

Before Kevin could say anything, Pilar started to move toward Anna like the Pink Panther cartoon tip-toeing in an over-exaggerated manner through the stacks of books.

"I think that might be a little obvious," Kevin laughed.

Pilar turned to him with her finger to her lips, "Shhhh." She then motioned for him to follow on her right as if they were a pair of spies.

Kevin decided to play along and made a Mission Impossible move and ducked and rolled right past her on the floor of the bookstore.

Pilar leaned against the book shelf next to her and peeked through to the other side. She saw Anna walking back towards where Kevin was rolling. She tried to make a motion for Kevin to stop but he was too caught up in the moment. Kevin made a sudden move around the corner of the shelf then popped himself up like a ninja and landed face to face with Anna.

"Ahhhh!" Anna screamed as she nearly lost her balance. Kevin reached for her arm and caught her. Pilar watched in horror.

"What the heck?" Anna asked once she was finally upright.

"I'm sorry," Kevin said. "This is so embarrassing. I'm a huge fan."

"Got to say this is the first time I've had a fan scare the shit out of me," Anna replied as she straightened her jacket.

"It was my fault," Pilar said as she approached. "We got a little carried away."

"It's fine," Anna replied. "You made my night more exciting than I thought it'd be here in the middle of America. Are you staying for the reading?"

"You're doing a reading? Tonight?" Kevin asked.

"I thought you said you were a fan," Anna replied.

"I am. I just didn't think you'd be at a bookstore in St. Paul," Kevin said.

"Oh, I wouldn't be here for my Broadway stuff. I wrote a children's book," Anna replied. "It's based off of the play Pretty Things."

"Really?" Pilar asked. "We saw that the last time we were in New York."

"We loved it," Kevin added.

"So, you're staying?" Anna asked.

"Of course," Pilar said. "It'll make his night." She knew how much this moment would mean to Kevin. Kevin grinned ear to ear. He was in awe of Pilar's thoughtfulness. As silly as his dreams sometimes seemed and as focused as Pilar was on her own career, it was comforting to know that she supported his interests.

Watching Anna talk about her creative process was inspiring to Kevin. Anna, who was known for her controversial marionette and puppet shows about politics was the last person he'd expect to write a children's book. But the book was incredibly written –smart, kind and gentle. Hearing Anna speak about pivoting to different creative outlets gave him a plethora of new ideas. After her talk, he approached her with a copy of the book to be signed.

"I would never have pinned you as a children's author," Kevin said. "But this is incredible."

"Sometimes you have to let your creativity take you where it's going to take you," Anna said. "I followed it here to this book and who knows where I'll go next."

Kevin let this sink in then said, "Thank you. I needed to hear that."

Anna nodded then signed his book *Follow it, don't resist it. Anna*

After the reading, Kevin couldn't thank Pilar enough for the night. "I'm really glad we got out of the house," he said.

"Me too," Pilar replied as she interlaced her fingers with Kevin's. "We needed that."

~~~

At the Riley house, Nola was the only one home. Earlier, her dad and Kulap had invited her to dinner since George was working, but Nola had declined the invitation. She needed a night of rest and knew that if she went out with her dad, he'd try to start a conversation about George and their relationship again and she wanted a moment to just be alone.

She decided to catch up on her favorite TV show, "Reed This." She had loved the streaming dramedy about the Reed kids growing up in a large extended family since the moment she read the pilot script. Her agent had sent her on an audition for the middle sister, and it had come down to her and three other girls. The producers liked Nola but decided to go in a different direction. Nola was devastated but it didn't make her give up, instead it pushed her to try harder. Three years later she had had many recurring roles in various shows but still had yet to land a big part.

Watching the show that night, she realized how much she missed LA and acting, so she decided to put on her own performance. She would watch a scene, memorize the lines, then act them out.

"No, Tom, that's not how it works in this family. We don't care that you're the youngest," Nola said taking on the persona of Louisa Reed. She paced across the living room, shaking her head at "Tom" who was really just the lamp in the corner.

"When Mom passed, this wasn't how the estate was supposed to be divided," Nola said in a dramatic fashion. Nola turned away from "Tom", trying to let him know how he had offended her.

"But what about my kids? I don't have the same sort of job you have," a mockingly deep voice said from behind Nola.

Nola turned around to find George standing next to the lamp. George flicked the light on and off, then fell to her hands and knees. "We can't live like this!"

Nola started laughing but played along. "This was your choice, Tom."

"But, Louisa!" George said in a completely over the top manner.

Nola couldn't control her laughing any longer. "I'm so glad you're a producer and not an actress."

George stood up with a grin. "I wasn't that bad."

"No. Not at all," Nola laughed. "Hey, what are you doing here, anyway?"

"Didn't you get my text?"

"I've been busy," Nola replied.

"I see that," George said. "Is Tom going to be okay?"

"Yes," Nola said. "In fact, we can find out right now if you want."

Nola snuggled into the couch, and George joined her. Before she turned "Reed This" back on Nola looked at her phone. "Awww, this is what you sent me?"

George had sent Nola a photo of her with her arm stretched out as if she was hugging someone. The text read: "Miss you! Coming home soon."

"I'm glad you're home," Nola said as she flipped through her phone. "Wait, you even sent a calendar invite?"

"I did," George replied.

The event was called "George and Nola snuggle time." George had scheduled it for an hour from the moment she sent the photo—6:45 pm. Nola was touched. When they had first begun dating George always sent her calendar invites. They were George's way of scheduling their time together. It seemed regimented and odd to Nola at first but after a while she grew to look forward to those invites. She hadn't received one in a long time and it made her happy to see it on her phone.

"So, are we going to do this?" George asked.

"Yes," Nola replied then breathed in the moment as George climbed into a spot behind Nola so that she could wrap her arms around her. Nola intertwined her fingers with George's.

It was good to be back in George's arms and feel connected to her not just through conversation but through moments like this where they could show each other affection with a gentle squeeze or strong arms wrapped around the other. "Reed This" played on the TV, but Nola was no longer paying attention. She was more interested in her wife. And George was pleased to be there too.

~~~

After dinner and the book signing, Pilar and Kevin returned home to find Nola and George fast asleep on the couch.

"Should we wake them," Pilar asked.

"Nah," Kevin said. "They look so peaceful there."

Kevin then tip-toed over to Pilar and grabbed her hand. He gently led her down the stairs. After their night together, he felt the closeness with Pilar building, and he didn't want it to stop. He quietly took her into their room then turned out the lights and softly began kissing her neck. Pilar smiled and melted into his arms. She knew where this was headed.

There would be no lengthy discussion—they had talked enough over the evening. This moment would be about the two of them connecting intimately. They both let themselves go and embraced the moment.

Afterwards, they lay in each other's arms.

"That was incredible," Pilar said.

Kevin smiled. "I didn't know how much I missed this."

"We're not going to wait that long again, are we?" Pilar asked as she placed her head on Kevin's chest. With work and school, it had been a while since they'd had sex.

"Nope," Kevin said. "I think we should do this again next Saturday."

"Which part? The bookstore or…," Pilar asked.

"Both," Kevin replied as he kissed the top of her head and held her closer. She nuzzled into the space between his chin and chest and listened happily as Kevin's heart beat against her cheek. It was moments like these that made her feel incredibly connected to her husband and she was grateful that they both cared enough to make them happen.

Chapter 10

Podcast #10
Assumptions of Negative Intent
Trigger Conflict

"One universal thing that happens during conflict is the common problem of making 'assumptions of negative intent' which frequently serve as an initial trigger point for so many conflicts.

As can easily happen in any relationship, one may drop the ball or do something to hurt the other person's feelings. For example, one partner might say: When you didn't call me last night while on your trip as you promised, I felt that you really didn't love me.' The other partner then might become defensive and say: 'how can you possibly think I really don't love you after all of the things that I've done for you and the commitment I've shown to you!' Further argument then might ensue with no real ownership or healing ever occurring for the injured feelings. Unfortunately the discussion has shifted from the inarguable specific negative behavior of 'failure to call as promised' to a defensive argument regarding the assumption: "you really don't love me."

Sound familiar? Has anything ever happened like this in your relationship?
None of us are taught how to communicate in a more precise way what the negative behavior is that's upsetting us. We tend to project a broader negative assumption with inflammatory elements fueling

a more defensive argument. This circular pattern caused by assumptions occurs in most relationships and makes it virtually impossible to ever really resolve any conflict. But there are ways to put a stop to this."

"I swear," Heather started. "He never listens to me. It's like he doesn't care."

"I care," Daniel replied. "I made one little mistake. We all make mistakes. Why does that mean I don't care?" Daniel asked in frustration.

Heather turned to Dr. Riley to explain, "He forgot to pick our daughter up from ballet practice."

"I was late. I didn't forget her," Daniel sighed.

"You forgot. Which made you late," Heather replied. "There's a difference."

"She was fine," Daniel said. "It wasn't a big deal. In fact, she liked it. The teacher let her dance with the older girls until I got there."

"That's not the point," Heather said with a sigh. "I asked you to pick her up so that I could stay late at work to finish my proposal."

"And I still picked her up, didn't I?" Daniel said.

"Yeah, but I still had to worry and step away from work. I don't know why you always think your work is more important than mine."

"I don't," Daniel replied.

"That's not how you act," Heather replied.

"See," Daniel said as he turned to Dr. Riley. "It's just like you said in your podcast this week. She always assumes the worst."

Dr. Riley nodded as he made a note in his notepad. He could see that the Greens had entered into a pattern of negative assumptions.

"What if I told you, you were right," Dr. Riley said to Daniel.

"I'd say, thank you," Daniel replied with a look to Heather that said *see!* Heather crossed her arms over her chest and Dr. Riley turned to address her.

"Heather, you did assume the worst," Dr. Riley said. "But you're correct too. You have a right to be upset and hurt."

This time, Heather shot Daniel a look. "See, I told you so," Heather said.

"Just because she's upset it doesn't mean she can attack my character," Daniel said.

"I didn't attack your character," Heather said.

"That's what it felt like. You do it a lot," Daniel started. "I do something wrong and suddenly everything's wrong."

"Hold on," Dr. Riley said. "Let's slow down. Daniel, I know you care about Heather, so let's start there."

"Of course, I care," Daniel said. "If I didn't care I would just be off doing whatever I wanted. I got caught up in work. That doesn't mean I forgot that she asked me to get our daughter. It means I got distracted. We all do."

"This is true," Dr. Riley said. "However, when we come from a place of assuming negative intent our feelings are overamplified. And that's what happened here. Heather, when Daniel didn't pick up your daughter, what did you think?"

"I felt like he did it on purpose. I felt like he didn't care enough about me or my work to put any of my needs ahead of his own," Heather said.

"And is this how you felt, Daniel?" Dr. Riley asked.

"No," Daniel said. "That never even crossed my mind. I really did just forget."

"Did you think of this simple alternative?" Dr. Riley asked Heather.

"No," Heather said softly. She hadn't considered it at all. She was used to Daniel forgetting things and at this point she operated from a place of assuming he was doing it out of spite.

"When you were upset that he didn't pick her up, you had every right to be upset, however, making the assumption that he did it because he didn't care is just that—an assumption," Dr. Riley said in a calming voice.

"I can see how that's true," Heather admitted. "I guess I just get so frustrated because I feel like this kind of thing happens a lot."

"Making assumptions is normal," Dr. Riley said. "I've seen the same thing happen over and over again in relationships. In fact, it's one of the primary factors behind conflict that festers, grows, and then erupts into serious arguments. When that happens, the argument gets high-jacked away from focusing on the specific negative behavior, like forgetting your daughter, and veers off to the highly debatable assumptions, that Daniel did it out of spite. He then reacts with defensiveness to those assumptions feeling his character was being attacked."

"You couldn't have said it any better," Daniel said. "This is exactly what we do. So, how do we get away from it?"

"Well, first, instead of making generalized, projected assumptions of intent it's better to stick directly with the behavior. Which, in this case, is forgetting to pick up your daughter. For which, Heather should address in the Softly Specific manner."

"Okay," Heather said. "So, it's okay to tell him what went wrong and ask him to change the behavior for next time?"

"Yes, as long as you don't generalize and make sweeping statements," Dr. Riley said then looked to Daniel for his response.

"And, next time I'll apologize for the thing I did wrong and take ownership of it," Daniel said.

"Good," Dr. Riley said. "When both partners recognize that the use of assumptions creates fuel to burn the fire of arguments you can get somewhere."

Daniel and Heather looked at each other in apology.

"I would never purposely forget our daughter," Daniel said.

"I know that," Heather replied. "And I'll remember that as long as you try not to explain things away each time."

"Deal," Daniel said.

Dr. Riley paused for a second then went on to state, "Remember this applies to both of you and the work goes both ways. It's not only Heather who has to stop from making assumptions it's you too, Daniel. You each need to be highly aware and cautious about your own tendency within yourself to make assumptions that fan the flame of conflict. And you must recognize that it will be hard for the other to accept ownership and apologize when you have made assumptions for which they may naturally become defensive."

Daniel and Heather nodded their heads in understanding.

"It will help if you both remember to slow down and ask, 'what did I do or say that made you unhappy?' when the other is upset instead of defending yourselves and feeling like it's an attack on your characters," Dr. Riley added.

"So we need to make sure that we talk about the specific thing that made us mad and not the assumption?" Heather added.

Dr. Riley nodded. The Greens were back on the right track. "So, can you agree to co-coach each other whenever you see assumptions being made since it's so common for this to occur in all relationships?"

"Yes," they both replied.

Dr. Riley smiled and closed his notebook. He then sent the Greens on their way to continue their work on co-coaching each other in their relationship.

~~~

The next morning Dr. Steve was reading the paper in the living room when the sound of a slamming door startled him. He looked up and saw Nola storming down the steps of the back patio. Dr. Steve arose from his seat and was about to follow her when George came running in.

"Did she go that way?" George asked pointing out the kitchen door. Dr. Steve nodded yes then took a step towards her.

"Don't worry, Dad, I'm going to fix this," George said as she opened the door. "We're just having a little spat. I did a bad thing and Nola's making assumptions. But clearly, I love her, so we'll be all good in no time."

"Okay, George, I'll be here making some coffee if you need me," he said as he stepped back.

"Thanks," George replied as she ran off down the steps and towards the dock on the lake.

Dr. Steve watched from the kitchen as George approached Nola. He could tell from afar that they were having a heated discussion. He turned to tend to the coffee. Though his natural inclination was to run and help, he knew this was something they needed to solve as a couple.

As Dr. Steve poured himself a cup of coffee, Kulap entered the kitchen. "What was all that commotion?"

"Nothing much. Just the kids," Dr. Steve said as he looked towards the lake.

Kulap peered out the window and saw George and Nola. "Those two okay?"

Dr. Steve nodded as he watched George and Nola hug. "They are now."

"Good," Kulap said then grabbed her own cup of coffee. "Because I was hoping we could go for a walk together before your first session."

"We absolutely can," Dr. Steve said. Over the last week, he and Kulap had recommitted to focusing on each other's needs and making time for one another. He liked taking walks with his wife and talking along the way. It was helping them re-establish their alone time together since the adult children had moved back home.

"The other kids gone for the day?" Kulap asked.

Dr. Steve nodded. Kevin and Pilar had left early that morning for the university. They were both in good spirits when they left, and this made Dr. Steve happy. Having his kids content made him feel free to spend time on his own relationship and that was something he appreciated.

"Ready?" Dr. Steve said as he finished his coffee and opened the back door so they could head out for their walk.

"Yep," Kulap said as she ducked under his arm and walked towards the steps. Dr. Steve followed. At the bottom of the staircase, they were about to make a sharp turn and head west along the lake, when they walked straight into Chet.

"I was hoping I'd run into you," Chet said excitedly.

"This is my house Chet. Odds of that happening were pretty high," Dr. Steve replied.

"I know. That's why I'm here," Chet said. "I really need to talk to you about Bree."

"Maybe you and I could schedule some time to talk later today. Just the two of us," Dr. Steve said.

"Oh, it's fine if Kulap stays." Chet said as he stood with them.

"Uh, Chet, we were on our way out for a walk together. Kulap and I," Dr. Steve said, trying to reiterate that this was their alone time.

"I see," Chet said as he turned to Kulap. "But you've been so great on those Instagram appearances I feel like you could provide a much needed female perspective here."

Kulap looked at Dr. Steve as if to say, *can you help here?*

"Chet, I don't know," Dr. Steve started. "I think it's better if we schedule our own time." Kulap sighed a sigh of relief, but Chet wasn't giving up.

"Did I mention how amazing you've been looking lately, Kulap. I feel like you're aging backwards," Chet said in a syrupy sweet voice.

This piqued Kulap's interest. "Really?"

"Oh my gosh, yes. Keep doing whatever you're doing," Chet replied as he eyed her up and down.

"Well, thank you. I will," Kulap said.

"Chet, how about one p.m. today. We can talk then," Dr. Steve said, hoping to scurry Chet along.

"It's okay, he can walk with us," Kulap said. Dr. Steve gave her a look like, *are you sure?* "Look at him. The man's wearing crocs. He clearly needs help."

"Is that why I'm having such problems?" Chet said as he looked down at his worn orange rubber shoes.

"I have a feeling it might be something else," Dr. Steve replied.

Chet sighed. "All right. Lay it on me, doc."

The three of them began their walk around the lake as Dr. Steve started to ask more questions.

~~~

That afternoon, Kevin met with his drama professor. After the reading he'd gone to with Pilar the week before, he'd had an epiphany about his own career. He wanted to do something more than simply a dinner theatre. With the help of his professor, he developed a new plan that incorporated puppets and could come to fruition much sooner. After the meeting, Kevin walked with a spring in his step through campus. As he walked through the main quad, he caught a glimpse of Pilar's dark hair amongst the sea of students headed to lunch. He quickly made his way through the crowd. He wanted to tell her about his meeting and have her share in his excitement.

"Hey," Kevin said as he walked straight up to her. Pilar turned with a start. She was in mid-conversation with a tall guy with sandy blonde hair.

"Kevin!" Pilar exclaimed as she turned from the blonde. She was surprised to see him. She paused for a moment to collect herself then remembered, "Trevor, this is Kevin. Kevin, this is Trevor."

Trevor held out his hand and the two greeted each other. "Hi," Kevin said.

"I'm really glad we finally get to meet," Trevor said.

"You are?" Kevin asked in a surprised tone.

"Yeah. I mean if you two are going to move in with me, I at least got to make sure we can be bros, right?" Trevor said with a pat on the back.

"Yeah, right," Kevin responded then realized, "Oh, you must be the guy with the house and an extra room." Kevin turned to Pilar. "I didn't know we were still considering it."

"Of course, we are," she said. "We can't live at your dad's forever."

Kevin became quiet. He didn't know what to say. Clearly, Pilar had not really heard him when they'd previously discussed the prospect of moving into Trevor's house. When he'd said that it was better for them to remain at his dad's house, he thought that was the end of the conversation. He thought Pilar was on the same page, but now he felt like he was being thrown under the bus.

"Dude, we should grab a drink one day," Trevor said.

"Sure," Kevin replied with hesitation. The whole situation made him feel weird.

"Unless, you don't drink, then we can get a coffee," Trevor replied.

"No, he drinks. We can all get a drink one day. In fact, let's do it Thursday night," Pilar said.

"What about—," Kevin started but Pilar cut him off.

"We can push that to Friday," Pilar replied. They had made plans to do dinner with Nola and George on Thursday, but Pilar thought this was more important. The way she saw it they had the opportunity to be with Nola and George every day. They could put them off for one night.

"This will be great," Trevor began. "You guys can come over and check out the place and then we can walk over to Finn's and grab a pint."

"It'll be *real* great," Kevin said with a look to Pilar.

"Fantastic, man," Trevor replied with a high-five. Kevin put up his hand for a weak slap back. Pilar took note.

"We got to go," she said. "Our next class is in ten minutes."

"Okay. I'll see you back at the car at six?" Kevin asked.

"Actually," Pilar began. "We've got a group project we're working on and Trevor said he wouldn't mind giving me a ride home tonight."

"Really? I don't mind coming back," Kevin said.

"It's no problem," Trevor replied.

"I'll see you later," Pilar said before Kevin could say anymore. She gave him a quick kiss on the cheek then headed off to class.

Kevin walked back to the car but felt odd about it. What had just happened? Not only had Pilar just steamrolled him with the whole conversation about moving in with Trevor but it also made him uncomfortable how much she had ignored his feelings to tend to Trevor's. He had had such a good day working on his future plans but those few minutes with Trevor had really thrown him off.

On the car ride home, Kevin stewed in his own thoughts. Was Pilar mad at him? Why did she always have a tendency to blow him off when she was around her colleagues? It was as if she didn't care about him. Was he not good enough for her anymore? She was smart and accomplished and what was he? A waiter with a pipedream? Kevin felt pretty low, but then he remembered how inspired he had been after the meeting with his professor. He had a lot to offer the world and if Pilar couldn't see it, then oh well, he thought.

Kevin continued to drive towards home. He was fired up and turned on the stereo only to realize it was connected to his phone. Immediately, his dad's podcast started playing.

"As can easily happen in a relationship, your partner may drop the ball or do something to hurt your feelings. However, you must be careful to not make an incorrect assumption about the intention behind their behavior," Dr. Steve's voice echoed through the car. Kevin was about to turn it off, but something told him to listen further. He let the podcast continue on. "In this case, you need to first think about what your partner's specific negative behavior is that upset you."

Kevin took note of this and decided that he would have a talk with Pilar that evening when Trevor dropped her off. He knew he needed to tell her how hurt he was by their conversation. Quickly forgetting everything he'd just learned from the podcast he began to craft everything he would say to her that night, "Why don't you love me enough to think about my feelings? Why do you always make plans without consulting me, it's like you don't care about my opinion at all?"

He continued on with this rant in his head. "Don't you love me?" He was fired up and ready to face Pilar that evening but suddenly he was brought back to the sound of his dad's voice dropping another relationship gem over the podcast.

"For the person delivering the feedback, it's also very important to watch out when making assumptions and learn to first check them out, such as saying, "I'm assuming that you said or did this because of XYZ. Is that correct?" Couples who learn this skill to check out the validity of their assumptions quickly discover that those assumptions, often of negative intention, are frequently incorrect."

Kevin sighed. He realized that everything he had planned to say in his head was a giant assumption. Deep down he understood that Pilar loved him, but still, he was upset and he would have to figure out a way to bring it up.

~~~

At nine that evening, Pilar finally returned home. Kevin was in bed reading a book on entrepreneurship. By that point he had calmed down and was ready to have a composed conversation with Pilar following his dad's pillars of advice. However, Pilar was in a different state.

"What was that all about today?" Pilar asked as she flung her coat onto the chair in the corner of the room.

"You don't know? Come on," Kevin reflexively responded. He had meant to be soft and specific but Pilar's tone threw him off and he was already on the defensive.

"I thought we'd agreed to stay at my dad's for at least the rest of the semester," Kevin said. "And then all of a sudden you're telling Trevor we're still in for his place?"

"Did we agree to that? Because I don't remember that specifically," Pilar said as she kicked off her shoes.

"You always do that," Kevin replied as he sat up in bed. "It's like you don't care about my input," Kevin said without thinking.

"What do you mean?" Pilar said. "Of course, I do. I value everything you say."

"Obviously not everything," Kevin said. "Or we wouldn't be having this conversation."

Pilar shrugged her shoulders and turned her back to him. Kevin was incredibly upset and getting angrier by the minute. But when he heard his dad's footsteps from upstairs he was reminded of the words of the podcast.

He took a deep breath. "Okay, let me back this up," he said in a calm manner. "I made the assumption that you don't really care about my feelings and you think you know better than me and that's why you told Trevor that we were still contemplating moving in with him. Is that correct?"

Pilar finally paused. "No, not at all," she said. "I told Trevor we were still thinking about it because I didn't want him to give the room to someone else in case we changed our minds."

"Why would we do that?" Kevin asked.

"I don't know. I just wanted us to have a back-up plan so that we didn't feel stuck," Pilar admitted.

"Are you feeling stuck?" Kevin asked out of genuine concern. He hadn't even thought of that before.

"Not stuck, but I miss the life we had in D.C. And last week after going downtown to St. Paul and going to the bookstore and the restaurant just the two of us, made me realize that I missed our independence. I love your dad and your sister, and even Kulap and George but it's a lot sometimes. Especially after being in school all day."

Kevin took this all in. He didn't know how Pilar had truly been feeling. "I can better understand you now," Kevin said. "I was making an assumption that you were keeping Trevor's place as an option to spite me. I can see how having a back-up plan is a good idea."

"Thank you," Pilar said. "I'm glad you recognize that."

"It's no problem," Kevin said. "However, I do want to point out that it did bother me that you agreed to drinks on Thursday without talking with me."

"I'm sorry," Pilar said. "I should've asked first. You're right. I know we had plans with your sister. I can reschedule with Trevor."

"Thanks," Kevin said. "That would mean a lot to me."

"I'm happy to do it. And I promise not to make plans without asking you again," Pilar reassured him.

"And I promise not to make assumptions," Kevin added.

Pilar leaned down and kissed him. "I think your dad would be proud of how we just handled that situation," she said.

"He would be," Kevin replied then thought about how maybe it was a good thing they were living at home. If he weren't there he probably would've let the words of his dad's podcast pass through one ear and out the other, but knowing he was upstairs served as a constant reminder to take the extra steps with his wife, speak in nicer, softer ways, ask questions and truly listen.

"Can we go to bed now?" Pilar asked. "I'm exhausted."

"Me too," Kevin said as he moved over and patted the bed. Pilar relaxed into the spot next to him and he wrapped his arms around her.

She whispered in his ear, "I love it that we're learning to talk through things so much better now."

He replied back, "Me too, It feels great! Let's always talk in this open softer way."

Pilar nodded her head and snuggled in closer. Slowly they drifted off to sleep.

Chapter 11

Podcast #11
Effective Communication Principles Couples
Never Learn

"Communication is at the heart of all problems that couples encounter. Learning the skill of clear, concise communication is imperative and none of us are taught this in our society. Couples in their conversations with one another tend to not answer questions directly, veer off onto loosely associated tangential topics, fail to clarify exactly what they are saying, get defensive, and talk in circles losing focus over what they actually started talking about. And they too often never come to any helpful resolution. So, here are the Five Key Skills in communication to be able to discuss any topic whether it be mundane responsibilities of home life, differences of opinion about a myriad of life issues, or deeper sharing of feelings.

　　1) Listen non-defensively
　　2) Clarify what each other is saying
　　3) Make direct requests
　　4) Stay on topic
　　5) Come to agreement"

"We're going to work on things a little differently today," Dr. Riley said as the Greens settled into their spots on his office couch. "I want you guys to think about a disagreement you've had recently, and we'll talk through it."

"We've been in therapy for months now. What makes you think we've had a disagreement?" Daniel joked.

Heather playfully slapped his arm. "He's kidding," she said.

"I know," Dr. Riley replied. "So, is there something you can remember where your communication felt completely off or got waylaid?"

Heather took a deep breath then began, "Yeah. I would say two weekends ago is a good example."

"Oh, yeah," Daniel said softly as he remembered their argument.

"I really messed up," Heather began. "Daniel had made plans for us to go to this pop-up drive-in theater that was opening for one weekend only. He tried to surprise me and I kind of blew it."

"Kind of?" Daniel said thinking back to that weekend. "We didn't get to go," he told Dr. Riley.

"What happened?" Dr. Riley asked.

"Well, he never makes plans and all of a sudden he did. So, I had no clue he wanted me home for a surprise date," Heather began.

"It's kind of hard to make it a surprise if you tell someone exactly what's happening," Daniel said in his defense.

"Right, but if 199 times out of 200 you tell me you want me to be home at a certain time and it's never made a difference before, how am I supposed to know that on the 200th time timing makes a difference?" Heather explained.

Daniel sighed and turned to Dr. Riley. "And this is exactly what happened when we tried to make it to the show," he said referencing the way Heather was responding in a defensive way.

"I don't know why, but I always want to explain myself," Heather said.

"Which is what I wanted to work on with you both today," Dr. Riley said. "I would like to go over some absolutely important skills of effective communication that none of us are taught in our society. We've worked on establishing your NRP's and your Love Needs and Co-Coaching one another in a Softly-Specific manner, but there are the five things to remember when you're faced with a moment where it feels difficult to get yourselves on the same page. The first is remembering to listen non-defensively."

Heather nodded in agreement. "Intellectually, I know I should listen and not get defensive, but in the moment it's hard to do," she said. "I think it comes back to holding on to things from the past. I'm pretty sure I still have some resentment when Daniel asks me to be home at a certain time. It feels too controlling. Clearly, that was not his intention that day, but that's what made it difficult for me in that moment."

"I can see that," Daniel said. He knew how much his wife valued her independence and he respected that. "I think I could have been clearer about why I wanted her home without blowing the surprise."

"Clarification is the second key to effective communication," Dr. Riley said. "Making sure that you don't speak in generalizations and that you each ask each other questions to clarify anything you don't fully understand."

"I mean obviously this was a bit of a misunderstanding, but if I had just said I have a surprise for you, can you be home at 6pm after your pedicure and time with your friends that probably would've been much better," Daniel said.

"Yes," Heather said. "If you'd said that, I would've been home exactly at six."

"But instead he said what?" Dr. Riley asked.

"Instead, he talked about how he had worked a long week and we hadn't spent enough time with each other and he finally had free time and wanted to spend it with me," Heather replied.

"How did that sit with you?" Dr. Riley asked.

"Not well," Heather said. "In my mind it felt like he was trying to make up for the fact that he didn't prioritize us all week and now he was asking me to give up my scheduled activity with my friends for him. It didn't seem fair," Heather replied.

Daniel sighed. He had no clue this was what was behind Heather's defensiveness. "I didn't realize all of that had gone through your head," he said.

Heather looked at him directly in the eyes. "It did," she replied.

"This is another great example where you both could've clarified your responses and your feelings in a more direct way," Dr. Riley added.

"For sure," Heather said realizing that adding a simple explanation to clarify how she felt would've helped the situation.

"And from there you could've gone on to the next step of effective communication and honed your skill of making a request," Dr. Riley said.

"Instead of speaking in generalizations, you both could've asked for a simple change in behavior. Daniel, you could've said, I know you have this event planned with your friends, but it would mean a lot to me if you came home a bit early because I have a surprise for you that's time sensitive."

"I would've responded much better to that," Heather said. "And probably wouldn't have been so defensive and righteous. It also probably wouldn't have escalated to where it did."

"And where did it go?" Dr. Riley asked.

"Oh, I went on a total tangent talking about how he's always working and how does he think it's okay for him to ask me to be home when he's never here," Heather said.

"So, you got off topic and also made negative assumptions?" Dr. Riley asked. Both Heather and Daniel nodded in agreement.

"It was a simple surprise date that turned into a big blow up," Daniel said. "I felt really bad because I knew she was mad about so much more, but I was also mad because I was trying to do something special."

"I know that now," Heather said. "And I'm sorry."

"Do you see how these steps are helpful?" Dr. Riley asked.

"Absolutely," Heather said. "There's one more step, right?"

"Yes," Dr. Riley replied. "That is learning to wrap up the conversation and come to an agreement. Here, you paraphrase back what you've each heard and come up with a plan to move forward."

"I've heard that I need to be clearer when I ask Heather to do something. I understand that she feels like I don't spend enough time with her during the week and that my work is a source of frustration," Daniel said.

Heather smiled and nodded. Daniel had understood the situation. Now it was her turn.

"I've heard that I need to not always jump to conclusions and listen non-defensively," Heather replied.

This time Daniel nodded and smiled.

"That was good," Dr. Riley said. "And obviously this was a fight over something that was going to be a great moment, so imagine if you had had a disagreement over something bigger."

"It wouldn't have been pretty," Daniel said. "But at least now, we can remember these five things and really talk through each problem."

"Definitely," Heather said as she reached over and squeezed Daniel's hand.

"It feels good to be able to get to this place so quickly now," Daniel added.

"Good," Dr. Riley said. "I want you to keep working on these skills. They may be easy to remember but you'd be surprised at how quickly couples forget them when they're in the middle of a disagreement."

"Oh, I think we know how that can happen," Daniel laughed. "But we're going to do our best. Right, babe?"

Heather smiled. "Right," she said, and they concluded their session that day feeling confident that the next disagreement they had would be more easily managed.

~~~

"Out, out, I need you all to get out," Kulap said. She was attempting to clean the kitchen but Nola and Kevin, who were making afternoon snacks, kept getting in her way. She'd tried to be nice and work around them, but after her twentieth time of having to ask them to move she'd had enough. "Get out of here!"

"We're gonna grab this plate and then we're out of your hair," Kevin said as he pulled a dish of homemade nachos out of the microwave and rushed towards the back door. Nola held the door open for him and they both took a seat around the table on the upstairs porch overlooking the lake.

"Okay, let's have a serious talk now," Kevin said. Nola took a deep breath to prepare. Was Kevin going to talk to her about her relationship and future too?

"The baby's dad is Tom Holland, right?"

Nola smiled with relief. "Spider Man? Really? You got to get better at this. You know I'm not a comic book fan."

Nola just shook her head. "You're not going to give up, are you?"

Kevin smiled. "What kind of brother would I be if I did?"

"The kind that keeps his nose out of other people's business," Nola said.

"Fine. You have a point. I'll let it go," Kevin said. "For today."

Nola sighed and shook her head. "So, do you think Kulap's okay?" Nola asked. She was worried that they'd really upset her.

"She's fine. Fine as anyone could be having their grown stepchildren living back at home," Kevin said as he popped a warm gooey nacho crisp into his mouth.

"It's kind of weird that we're both back here isn't it?" Nola said.

"It certainly wasn't my first choice of places to be in life at the age of twenty-seven," he replied.

"Me either," Nola said.

"How is everything going?" Kevin asked. "This is a lot of change for you at once. Getting married, moving home, having a baby."

"It's fine," Nola said as she picked at the skin around her thumb. He recognized the habit. It was one she had adopted at an early age. Whenever she talked about something that made her uncomfortable, she would fiddle with her thumb..

"So, it's not fine," Kevin said as he inched the plate of nachos closer to Nola.

Nola took a bite then waited a moment before responding. "George and I have been working through a lot of different things and no matter how much we communicate and do all the things we should do when trying to talk it out —you know, like following all of dad's suggestions for speaking in Softly Specific terms and clarifying what we want and listening non-defensively—I still have this sinking feeling in my gut that George is going to disappoint me."

"How?" Kevin asked.

"That's the thing. I don't know. And I don't even know if I'm being realistic. I brought it up the other day, but it came across too negative. I know she's trying, but I worry that she's never going to figure things out in life. She was a good producer in LA, but she messed that up with her pot farm. And, here she seems lost too. Which I guess we all are at this point. But I don't want to live here long term and I want to feel secure in our future."

"You still love her though, right?" Kevin asked.

"Of course," Nola said. "To be honest none of this would bother me if we weren't having a kid in less than a month."

"I could see how that would be a little scary," he said.

"Right? So maybe that's just heightening everything. Which is why I have to remind myself that every couple goes through things. She's never done anything unforgivable and she always means well. Maybe we just have to keep working on communicating more in the ways we are learning. Dad always said it takes time. I mean you and Pilar aren't perfect, are you?"

"No. We definitely are," Kevin smiled.

"Seriously though," Nola said.

"Seriously? We have our issues," Kevin replied. "But we talk openly and are getting through them with help from, I hate to admit it, a lot of what we've been learning in dad's podcasts."

"So, you like living here?" Nola asked.

"I like saving money and I think it'll help me when I launch my next step. But I know it bothers Pilar and that in turn bothers me. We've had some pretty heated discussions over it."

"You have?" Nola asked. She was surprised to hear this. In her mind, Kevin and Pilar had a strong, steady relationship.

"Yeah. We've worked through most of it. But somehow, I'm going to drinks tonight with her very attractive male classmate who wants us to move into his place," Kevin said.

"That seems..." Nola started.

"Weird?" Kevin asked.

"Yeah," Nola said.

"I don't think it's meant to be weird. I think it's like being in college and living with a bunch of people to save money, but yes, there is something that doesn't feel right about being married and moving into a guy's house with your wife."

"That doesn't seem like my dream scenario either," Nola said. "But I guess it could be worse."

"Really, how?" Kevin asked.

"You're asking someone who's living with her dad because her wife got busted and lost her lucrative job."

"I guess our live at home scenario isn't too bad," Kevin said. "I just hope I can be clear enough with Pilar after we check out Trevor's house tonight and let her know that I'm not comfortable with us moving in there."

Nola took one of the final nachos off the plate. "You'll be fine," she said.

"I hope you're right," Kevin said as he sat back in his chair and contemplated his next steps.

~~~

That evening, Kevin and Pilar arrived at Trevor's place near campus at six o'clock. In their short ride there they discussed their plan. This would just be some fun happy hour drinks with a classmate. Pilar agreed that she would tell Trevor that they were going to have to pass up living with him and that they would live with Kevin's dad at least until the end of the semester. In January, they'd reassess and consider moving out. Kevin thought this was a great compromise. They could save money for the next four months and they'd still have the option to move in later if they decided they'd had enough with Kulap and Dr. Steve. When they got to the house, they both felt like they were on the same page.

"Let's have fun tonight," Pilar said.

"Good idea," Kevin said. "We haven't spent time with anyone our age outside of our family in forever. It'll be nice to have a couple beers, maybe throw some darts and relax."

"I'm glad you agreed to do this," Pilar said.

"Me too," Kevin said. Just as Pilar was about to kiss Kevin, Trevor opened the front door and Pilar pulled away from her husband. Kevin took a step back and almost fell off the front stoop.

"Woah there, buddy, that excited to see me?" Trevor said in a deep but friendly voice. "Welcome," he said as he gave Pilar a giant hug and ignored Kevin. "Come in, come in," he said.

Trevor led the way as he brought them inside to give the grand tour.

"This is the kitchen," Trevor said as they entered a fully remodeled, bright and airy space. Trevor pointed to the stove. "That Viking range is amazing. I cooked a steak on there the other night and mmmm-mmm."

Pilar was in awe, running her fingers over the marble counter tops. Kevin was impressed. The house was quite spacious and nice. Definitely not like the college style living Kevin had been expecting.

"This is really amazing," Kevin said.

"If I wasn't returning to New York after graduation, I'd definitely consider buying the place. So, are you guys completely sold? We gonna be roomies?" Trevor asked.

"I don't know. I really like it, but..." Pilar said as she imagined herself having a peaceful morning coffee on the little porch off the back where their room would be. "Let us think about it some more."

Kevin eyed Pilar. This was definitely not what they had agreed upon in the car. Pilar shrugged and smiled. "You don't like it?"

Kevin was completely put on the spot. "It's great," Kevin said. "But what about what we talked about?"

"Ah, we'll figure it out," Pilar said then turned to Trevor. "Show us the local bar so we know what we'd be missing if we don't move in."

Trevor happily led them out the door and down the street. While he and Pilar talked about their classes, Kevin trailed behind. He didn't want to be the odd man out, but he didn't know how to confront Pilar in front of someone else. He knew he had to be direct and clear about what he wanted, but having Trevor there added a whole other layer he had to deal with.

Five minutes later they approached a small pub that looked like it belonged in an English countryside. "This place is adorable," Pilar said as they entered. "Look, Kevin, they even have darts."

"First round's on me," Trevor said as he headed to the bar.

Once Trevor was out of ear shot, Kevin turned to Pilar.

"What happened back there?" Kevin asked.

"Nothing. The place is awesome. That's all. I couldn't resist," Pilar said. Kevin shook his head. He was clearly upset. "Come on, let's enjoy the night. We can get into this later. Nothing's set in stone," Pilar said as she squeezed his hand.

"Fine," Kevin said. He couldn't deny the fact that the pub was a great hangout spot and he was looking forward to a night of letting loose and relaxing. He decided that he'd enjoy the evening and when they got home, they'd have a real discussion.

~~~

At the Riley house, Dr. Steve and Kulap had settled into bed for the evening. Kulap rolled over and turned to him with a serious look on her face. Dr. Steve knew that look, that was the look that said, 'we need to talk.'

"I need you to not get defensive," Kulap said.

"Okay," Dr. Steve replied in a soft tone. "What's bothering you?"

"The kids," Kulap said.

"Did something happen?" Dr. Steve asked out of genuine concern.

"Nothing particular. I miss my space. I miss us," she said as she settled into bed.

Dr. Steve sat up. He wanted to give his wife his full attention. "What do you mean by that? What is it you miss exactly?" he asked, looking for clarification.

"This is going to sound silly," Kulap said.

"Nothing's silly if it's bothering you," Dr. Steve replied.

"I want to be able to clean alone," Kulap said.

"But I thought you hate cleaning?" Dr. Steve said. In the past Kulap always complained about having to clean. It was her least favorite chore and she was constantly wondering why they couldn't simply hire someone to help out around the house. However, once they moved into their new home it became clear that they needed to cut back on extra expenses for a little bit until they built up their savings again. They had reached an agreement where her job was to clean a certain number of the rooms and Dr. Steve was in charge of the rest.

"I do, but it's also become this meditative thing for me," Kulap said. "And I don't have that right now because the kids are always around."

"Is that a true statement?" Dr. Steve asked asking her to not use general terms.

"Okay, they're not <u>always</u> around, but they do get in the way," Kulap said.

"How do they get in the way?" Dr. Steve asked. "They're adults. It's not like they're leaving their toys everywhere and constantly asking you to do things for them," Dr. Steve said as he remembered how much work it was for him to keep up with two young toddlers.

"I know that," Kulap said. "Confession?"

Dr. Steve nodded—go ahead.

"When I clean, I like to blast music, put on a bikini, and go to town. It's like my time to let go and be free," Kulap said.

"You own a bikini?" Dr. Steve asked.

"Yes, it makes me feel good when I'm alone," Kulap said. "Female empowerment."

"That's amazing. How can I help?"

"What if we sat the kids down and said every other Thursday was cleaning day and they had to be out of the house from 11am to 4pm," Kulap said.

Dr. Steve thought about it for a moment then said, "That sounds reasonable. I can agree to have that talk with them and make sure you have your time."

"Thank you," Kulap said as she leaned over and kissed him. "I'm glad we're able to talk about it and come to a good solution."

"Me too," Dr. Steve said as he pulled her in close to him. "Any chance I'm allowed home during those hours?" he asked.

"Didn't I just tell you this was about me?"

"I know but it sounds kind of sexy," Dr. Steve said as he nuzzled into her neck.

Kulap softened. "Okay. You can join me for the last hour. But you have to scrub the sinks," she said as she melted into his arms.

"Deal," Dr. Steve said with a smile. It was easy to agree to help around the house once he found out how important it was to her.

It was even more satisfying when Kulap said, "Can you tell I've been listening to your podcast on good communication? How did I do?"

Dr. Steve replied: "You are an excellent student, I give you an A plus!"

She then moved very close into him and whispered, "Good, now please do more than just imagine me in that bikini!" She draped herself around him and Dr. Steve slipped into a deep state of heavenly bliss. The only thought entering his mind was *it couldn't possibly get any better than this*!

~~~

When their rideshare dropped them off at the house, Pilar and Kevin were exhausted. It was almost eleven and they hadn't been out that late since they'd moved to Minnesota. They stumbled into the kitchen, grabbed giant glasses of water then made their way down to their bedroom.

After they had finished brushing their teeth and getting ready for bed, they both lay down next to one another.

"I know I'm going to pay for this tomorrow," Pilar said. "But that was fun."

"It was," Kevin said. Though he was still upset about the fact that Pilar had steamrolled their conversation with Trevor, he did have fun drinking beers and throwing darts.

"But?" Pilar prompted him.

"What do you mean, but?" he asked.

"Come on, I know you're not completely happy with the way I handled Trevor," she said.

"Well, we had agreed to a plan in the car ride over," Kevin said.

"We did," she replied. "But I didn't know how nice the place would be."

"Was it just the house?" Kevin asked.

"What do you mean?" Pilar asked.

"Trevor's awfully nice to you too," Kevin replied.

"Is that what you're really upset about?" Pilar asked sensing a hint of jealousy in Kevin.

"No. But it doesn't help," Kevin said.

"That's cute," Pilar said.

"What's cute about it?" Kevin asked, starting to get defensive. "There's nothing cute about another man hitting on your wife."

"He wasn't hitting on me," Pilar replied.

"Okay, but he was flirtatious," Kevin said.

"That's who he is. You saw him at the bar. He's like that with everyone," Pilar pointed out.

Kevin couldn't deny that truth. "You're right. I'm sorry. I liked the house too, but I still feel uncomfortable about moving in there."

"Okay," Pilar said. "Can you help me understand why? I always thought it was about the money, but I think it's more."

"I don't like the idea of my wife and I moving into a house with another man. It just feels weird," Kevin admitted.

"How so?" Pilar asked.

"I don't know. To me, once you're married you don't take on roommates," Kevin said.

"I can see that. But what about living with your dad and Kulap? Are they not our roommates too?"

"They're family," Kevin said. "There's a difference."

"I guess you're right, but still they're not my blood relatives. It's not as comfortable for me as it is for you," Pilar admitted.

Kevin sat for a moment and let this sink in. He hadn't heard Pilar voice it in this way before, but now he understood the hesitation she'd had all along. "I can see why that would bother you," Kevin said. "I guess I always just figured we were living here to save money and it was fine."

"In some ways it is," Pilar said. "But obviously after talking tonight we have different views on this."

Kevin nodded then admitted, "I didn't know how you felt, but now I see that your hesitation about living here wasn't just about me telling my dad that we were going to live with him last minute that made you feel awkward, it was that moving into a family home that wasn't your family's felt awkward."

"Exactly," Pilar said. She felt grateful that Kevin could listen to her and really understand what she was saying. "And, I didn't know that part of not wanting to move in with Trevor had more to do with your vision of our marriage and its boundaries than just saving money."

"Thanks for seeing that," Kevin said.

"Of course," Pilar said. "Though I have to admit it is nice to watch you get jealous. Makes me feel wanted."

"Oh, does it," Kevin said as he pulled her in close to him.

"It does," Pilar said as she snuggled her arms around his torso and intertwined her legs with his.

"I guess I should get jealous a little more often then," Kevin said as he began to kiss her neck. Pilar smiled and kissed him back. Then they held each other and stayed up an hour longer just talking, snuggling, and enjoying this very special moment until they drifted off into deep satisfying sleep.

Chapter 12

Podcast #12
Highly Developed Empathy and Listening Skill

"The ability to really listen and show empathy is at the heart of the deep connection between any two partners in a relationship. It's important to be able to share the daily stressors and feelings that arise from work, family, and other personal relationships. Each partner has a need to share the difficulties as well as the positive, joyous moments in life.

The problem is, none of us have been trained or educated in society in how to be empathetic and how to be a truly good listener, especially men. There is a gender related social conditioning factor that is at play for this difference between men and women. However, it's not just a male problem in being less skilled in empathy and listening, it also can hold true for many women.

But it's more frequently encountered in men where there is a powerful social conditioning for them to be problem solvers, strong and confident in their job, and to be ready to give solutions. They are not educated or trained in how to be empathetic.

So, let me introduce you to two skills that will help take any couple to the deepest level of emotional connection where you both feel really acknowledged and validated!"

Heather and Daniel arrived at Dr. Riley's office that day ready to work. They'd had a mini argument on the way to their appointment and they were both feeling frustrated. Dr. Riley could sense their irritation and immediately asked them what was going on.

"He's been doing that thing he does again," Heather said with a sigh.

"And what is that thing exactly?" Dr. Riley asked for clarification.

"You know, the one where he knows it all," Heather replied as she gave Daniel a sideways glance.

"Can you be more specific?" Dr. Riley prompted her.

"Yeah, because I'd like to know too," Daniel added then turned to Dr. Riley. "Our relationship hasn't been this good since we first started dating, yet she's been so weird lately."

"I haven't been weird," Heather retorted. "Just frustrated."

"And why is that?" Dr. Riley asked.

"I'll tell you why," Heather began. "Every night he gets to come home and vent about his long day at work and the things that went wrong and I listen to him and I support him. But, as soon as I mention one little thing that happened during my day that I didn't like, he goes off on a tangent and starts telling me what I should've done, or what I could do next, or what I should do in the future. It's like he doesn't even listen to me," Heather finished as she leaned back into the couch and shifted her body so that it was turned away from Daniel.

Dr. Riley had heard this complaint from many of his clients before. He understood where Heather was coming from. "I can see how that would be frustrating," he said.

"Right? I just want him to hear me out and let me vent," Heather replied. "I feel like he doesn't really listen. He only wants to add his two cents."

"I see," Dr. Riley said. "And what do you think about what Heather just stated, Daniel?"

"I understand that she's upset, but I'm a problem solver. I don't see what's wrong with offering suggestions," he replied. "If I hear her situation and I have a solution why can't I give it to her?"

"See? It's happening again," Heather said then turned to Daniel. "I'm not asking for advice. I'm asking you to just listen."

Dr. Riley could see that Daniel still wasn't understanding what Heather was asking for. He knew this because he'd seen it all too often. There was something very important Heather was missing in their relationship.

He looked at Daniel. "At work and in other life situations, solving problems is great. But here? When you jump to fixing things immediately without listening to your wife, you leave out one of the single most important things that makes a relationship good," Dr. Riley explained.

"And what's that?" Daniel asked with a huff.

"Empathy," Dr. Riley said then calmly continued on. "Would you like me to teach you in the next five minutes how to become a 21st-century enlightened husband who knows the secret to giving every woman the empathy she needs and wants so badly?"

Heather's eyes lit up and Daniel took notice. "If that'll fix this never-ending frustration then yes, tell me now," Daniel said.

Daniel sat at attention, ready to learn and Heather sat up as well. She was curious. Dr. Riley had been right about everything before and she couldn't wait to hear his method for addressing her husband's need to fix everything and never listen.

"First," Dr. Riley began. "When Heather comes to you at the end of a long day, you must give her your full attention with direct eye contact and no distractions. No looking at your cell phone, TV, or anywhere else."

"Okay," Daniel said as he turned and looked directly at his wife.

"Now, when she tells you what's been going on her life that has her frustrated, just listen and don't try to "fix" or give solutions," Dr. Riley said.

"I can definitely try," Daniel said. "But, I might need a bit of coaching here," he added.

"And, I think that Heather can remind you that she's not looking for a solution. Right?" Dr. Riley asked as he turned to Heather.

Heather smiled and nodded.

"Great. Now, when she's talking, you need to occasionally stop and ask a brief question or make a short comment that promotes further in-depth sharing on her part," Dr. Riley said.

"Okay, I'll do that" Daniel said.

"Next, and this is incredibly important, periodically make an empathy statement using one of the following three examples of empathic language: (1.) 'I can totally (or completely, really, or absolutely) understand why you would be feeling X in this situation of Z', (2.) 'I'm so sorry to hear you are feeling X and this is happening to you.' (3.) 'That must be really tough (or really rough, or hard),'" Dr. Riley said.

"Hold up," Daniel said as he brought out his phone. "I know you said no distractions, but I need to put these in my notes. Seems like the kind of thing every man should memorize."

Dr. Riley smiled. "Yes, actually, that's exactly what I was going to ask you to do."

Dr. Riley repeated the examples of empathy responses so that Daniel could take notes. After Daniel had gotten it all down, Dr. Riley went on to finish the method in which Daniel should communicate with Heather. "Once you've gotten this far in the conversation and you've spent a lot of time doing the four steps I mentioned, then and only then can you ask permission to see if Heather would be interested in any suggestions or advice that might be helpful."

"I think this might be difficult for me to remember how to always follow all these steps," Daniel said.

"Yes, it's an entirely new habit. It may not be easy. So you'll likely need Heather's continued co-coaching when you slip up," Dr. Riley said. "Will you be open to her coaching? And will you help him Heather?"

Both answered affirmatively. Then Heather added, "If you can do this for me it would make me so very happy. I would finally feel heard by you," Heather said.

Daniel heard her loud and clear and quickly replied, "I really do want to do this!".

"It'll take some practice, Daniel. But I'm sure you'll be successful if you really make it a priority. It's an exceedingly important love need for Heather as it is for most women.," Dr. Riley said. "You can become her 21st century enlightened husband!"

"I'll do my best!" Daniel said.

"I'm excited to hear you say that," Heather replied.

As they were now at the close of their session, Daniel said, "Thank you for another great session, I look forward to next week."

"As do I," Dr. Riley said as Daniel stood and reached out his hand to help Heather get up from the couch. The demeanor between the Greens had shifted drastically from the time they walked into his office until now. Dr. Riley smiled. It pleased him when his couples made genuine progress.

~~~

When Dr. Steve returned home from his sessions that day, he heard the roar of a boat engine down by the dock. As he walked around the house, Dr. Steve saw Chet's boat but there was no Chet. *Did something happen?* he thought. Dr. Steve took off running down the backyard slope towards the water. When he was within ten yards of the dock, he spotted Chet off to the side hunched next to a berm of shrubs.

"What are you doing?" Dr. Steve asked as he approached. Chet stood up and looked at him with a giant grin on his face.

"Digging for gold, basically," Chet said.

"What? There's no gold here," Dr. Steve replied.

"No, but there's this." Chet held up a giant marijuana leaf.

Dr. Steve reached out, grabbed the leaf, and began to inspect it. "Where did you get this?

Chet nodded towards a spot between two shrubs where several pot plants had begun to bloom. "I can't believe you've been holding out on me," Chet said. "Why didn't you tell me you were in the growing business?"

"I'm not," Dr. Steve said. "I don't know how those got there."

"I can take a guess," Chet replied as he looked back up at the house where George was sitting outside on the porch.

"You think she's been purposely growing them? No way," Dr. Steve said. "She's smarter than that."

"Well, somebody's been doing it," Chet said. "And it wasn't me."

Dr. Steve sighed. "Raincheck on the ride?" he asked. "I've got to go have an important conversation."

"Sure," Chet said with a shrug of his shoulders. "But you don't mind if I take this do you?" he asked as he took back the leaf from Dr. Steve's hand.

Dr. Steve brushed off his hands and shook his head. "I don't want to see you back here, though. And, I'm coming out here tonight with the lawnmower and some vinegar."

"Vinegar?" Chet asked confused.

"Kills weeds," Dr. Steve replied in a nonchalant manner as he walked off towards the house.

Once Dr. Steve was halfway back to the house, Chet turned around and grabbed a few more pot leaves before he hopped in his boat and drove away.

By the time the sound of Chet's engine had disappeared in the wind, Dr. Steve had made his way up the stairs to the porch.

"Hey, dad," George said as she looked up from the baby book she was reading. "No ride?"

"Not today," Dr. Steve replied as he took a seat on the chair across from her then folded his hands in front of him on the table.

"What's on your mind? You look a little perturbed," George said placing her book down on the table. George could tell he meant business.

"Actually, there's something I want to talk to you about," Dr. Steve said.

"Now this is a nice reversal in roles. Usually, I'm the one coming to you for advice," George said. "Tell me. What's going on?"

"Well, George, I found something down there in the shrubs and I don't want to make a judgment or assumption but I have a feeling you might know how it got there," Dr. Steve said.

"Sir, I'm not sure what you're talking about, maybe you can clarify," George replied. She had learned in working with Nola that it's always better to ask for clarification than to guess.

"I found pot, George," Dr. Steve said in a matter-of-fact manner.

"Like a joint?" George asked surprised. "'Cause I've been trying to make sure I throw those away. I hate when people litter," she said.

"No, George. I found a marijuana tree," Dr. Steve said with a concerned look. "Again, I don't want to make assumptions but if you're thinking about getting back in business this is really not the place."

Now George looked concerned. She didn't want Dr. Steve to think ill of her. "I definitely wouldn't do that here, and I made a promise to Nola that I would do anything to help our financial situation as long as it was on the up and up," she explained.

"That's what I thought," Dr. Steve said. "Which is why I'm coming to you first."

George took a moment to think about the situation. Then she wondered aloud, "Sir, when you say marijuana tree do you mean it was tall and skinny?"

"Not super tall," Dr. Steve replied.

"But not a bush?" George asked.

"Not really," he said. "Does that matter?"

George nodded as she sighed a sigh of relief and replied, "It does."

Dr. Steve gave her a quizzical look. "Really?"

"Yes. Because the farm bill of 2018 made hemp legal, which is good because I'm thinking that what you found down there was a hemp plant, not the kinda greenery that produces the wacky stuff. It's rare but sometimes they can grow from discarded dried marijuana which could've come from one of my joints."

"Well, that's good news," Dr. Steve replied.

"Kinda sorta," George said. "You see sir, I'm 99% positive that's a hemp plant but there's only one way to be certain and that's for me to dry it and smoke it. If I get high it's weed, if I don't it's hemp." George took a deep breath. Dr. Steve braced himself, then she continued, "So, I'm thinking you'd rather just have me remove it, correct?"

Dr. Steve let all of this information sink in then nodded. "Correct," Dr. Steve said.

"I'll get on that right away," George said as she moved to leave.

"Wait," Dr. Steve said. George paused and gritted her teeth. She was certain she was about to be reprimanded, but then Dr. Steve continued. "I'm really glad you're honoring your commitment to Nola," he said.

George relaxed with a smile. "You know, your work is helping us," she said. "Just yesterday, Nola was so upset about her birth plans. The doula we've been working with had sprung some new birthing method on her and she wasn't ready to accept that when things go down, they're likely to be unpredictable."

"Giving birth can be a scary time," Dr. Steve said remembering how nervous Nola's mom was before she gave birth.

"I know, that's what I said to her," George said. "You'd be really proud of me. I sat across from her, put away my phone, turned off the TV and said let's talk. And we did. And I listened and I didn't try to fix the situation, even though I wanted so badly to tell her all the things we could tell the doula, or even fire her if we wanted. But I didn't. Instead, I told Nola that I understood her fear. That this was a difficult time. I let her say everything she needed to say. And, for once, she actually turned to me after our conversation and thanked me."

"That's great," Dr. Steve said, recognizing that George had been working hard on her empathy skills. "So things are good now?" Dr. Steve asked.

George smiled. "They are. I'm headed to see the doula tomorrow to give her a piece of my mind," George said as she made a fist and shook it like she was ready for confrontation.

"Can I offer you another piece of advice?" Dr. Steve asked.

George nodded. She appreciated how knowledgeable Dr. Steve was and openly accepted his guidance.

"When you go see the doula, might I suggest you offer her a bit of empathy as well," Dr. Steve said.

"How so? I mean, I'm going there to tell her that what she did really upset my wife," George explained.

"And that's admirable and I'm sure Nola will appreciate it. But there's another part of the empathetic listening skills that I didn't fully go into in my podcast this week, but I believe it'll help you. I refer to it as Higher-Level Listening for Merit," Dr. Steve began.

"I like the sound of it," George said. "Go on."

"It's really effective, not just in romantic relationships, but also in professional ones as well. It involves the capability of suspending your own bias about one's opinion on any matter of discussion, and truly listening in an unbiased way to what the other person is saying."

"Say what?" George asked.

"It's like sitting back and listening with no distractions, but instead of just listening to let someone vent and to show your empathy, here you're listening to find merit in some part of what they're saying," Dr. Steve explained.

"Okay," George said. "So, I'm there to see if what she said about the birth plan makes sense?"

"Yes," Dr. Steve said. "Most people hold strongly to their own opinions, have a bias about it when they begin a discussion, and are not very open. In particular, they are not intentionally looking for some facet of what's being expressed that is positive to validate or acknowledge."

"That makes sense," George said. "I mean, I know the doula has experience, but she doesn't know Nola the way I do and so, you're right I was going to go in there with a bias to tell her exactly how she should've handled the situation. But I think I need to hear her out and help Nola do the same."

"Exactly. I'm glad you understand," Dr. Steve said. "And this doesn't just apply to the situation with the doula. Acknowledging the merit in your partner's point of view is important when discussing differences of opinion on all issues."

"I'm going to remember that," George said. "Especially with the baby coming. You know we both have differing opinions on how this is going to work and how we're going to parent together."

"Every couple has the same issues, but I'm happy to hear that you're really working on this," Dr. Steve said.

"You know, as weird as this whole living with my wife's family thing has been, it's actually been really nice living here with you," George said with a smile. Dr. Steve smiled back at her. As awkward as it was, he did enjoy having her and Nola around. It made him feel useful and it reinforced his belief that his Co-coaching methods could really help anyone in any relationship. But more than that, he was happy that he was able to help his adult daughter in a way that most parents couldn't and that was something he was proud of.

~~~

George and Nola sat in the cozy office of their doula the next day waiting for her to arrive. They had gotten there early and were using these few minutes to check-in with one another.

"Do you want me to talk, or do you want to do it?" George asked. She wanted to be respectful of Nola's concerns and didn't want to overstep her boundaries.

"I think we should both feel free to say what we need to say," Nola said.

"Okay. That sounds good," George said with a smile. She was thankful that Dr. Steve had talked her through how to listen to the doula without bias and was confident that the appointment would go well.

When the doula walked in, Nola and George both sat at attention.

"How are you feeling today?" the doula asked Nola.

"Good," Nola said. "I'm starting to get more back pain, but that's normal, right?"

The doula nodded. "It is. So, what can I help you guys with today? I know you have some questions about what we went over before."

"I do," Nola began then took a deep breath. "But first I want to say that I'm feeling uncomfortable about all of these options and things that could go wrong. Like, are they going to have to induce me or break my water, or what if the cord is wrapped up around the baby's neck? I feel like I've gotten so much information at this point that I don't know what to do." Nola sat back. She was clearly overwhelmed. George noticed that Nola's hands were shaking. She reached over and placed her hand on top of Nola's.

"These are all valid concerns," the doula said. "Which is why I brought everything up the other day. It's important that you know what could possibly go on during the birth. It helps you prepare."

Nola's hands started shaking even more. Seeing Nola upset, upset George. George instinctively made a move. "Do we really need to know everything?" George asked.

"I like my patients to be fully informed," the doula said. Nola squeezed George's hand to indicate that it was fine, then gathered the courage to speak up.

"I'm trying to be prepared but I'm overwhelmed. I think I need you to slow it down," Nola said.

"I can do that," the doula responded. "Which part would you like to discuss? The episiotomy? I know you had trouble hearing that last time we were together."

"I guess. Sure, I don't know," Nola said. George could sense how uncomfortable Nola was, but she was doing her best to listen to the doula.

"Okay, well, if the baby's head is bigger than expected, there's a possibility that an incision will need to be made," the doula began.

"A what?" George asked. She cringed at the thought of a knife entering Nola's skin and couldn't help herself, "You're scaring my wife."

"I'm not scared," Nola said then turned to the doula. "It's okay. Keep going."

The doula continued on, but George was already feeling triggered and sat on edge. "It's a simple procedure, and Nola, you'll be numb. Even if you weren't, it's likely the pain of the incision wouldn't really compare to the pain of the contractions," the doula said.

This level of detail set George off. "Really?" George exclaimed. "That's how you want to present this?"

"Yes," the doula said. "This is how it works."

Nola looked over at George with a *please don't do this now* look, but George was already perturbed.

"You can't say something like that," George said. "That's like me getting on a plane and the flight attendant telling me exactly how a water landing is going to happen. I don't need to know gory details. I just need to know where my flotation device is."

"It's okay," Nola said. "I understand that this is not going to be easy or comfortable. I need to hear this."

George turned to her wife and gave her full attention. "Sure," George replied. "But there's a way to say it that's a little more graceful."

"I don't know," Nola said as she shook her head. "I think that's what she already tried, and I didn't grasp it all," Nola finished.

"It's true," the doula said. "This is normally how the process works."

"Then I don't think this is a good process," George said. She was becoming more and more frustrated by the minute.

The doula remained calm. "I can assure you, that all the feelings you're feeling right now are normal. And I am doing everything I've done for the last seventy-three babies I've helped coach into this world."

George shook her head. She was having a hard time believing that this was the way birth prep was supposed to go. When she was producing in

Hollywood, she always had to lay out the straight facts, that was a given, but when it came to bringing life into the world, it felt like there had to be a softer, gentler approach. "I still think there's a better way," George said.

"You're not listening," Nola said with a raised voice.

"Yes. I am. I heard everything she said," George replied in a defensive manner.

"No. You're not listening to me," Nola said.

This hit George hard. She had done it again. She had failed to truly listen to what Nola was saying. She took a pause, remembered what Dr. Steve had said, then told Nola, "You're right. How do you want this to go?"

"I need to hear everything she has to say. Even the difficult parts," Nola said.

Even though George felt like this was the wrong approach, she had to think about what Nola needed. "Okay," George said then turned to the doula. "I'm sorry. You can continue on."

"It's all right," the doula said. "This is a stressful time. There are going to be moments where you feel out of control and want to assert yourself." The doula then turned to Nola. "Are you ready for me to move forward?"

Nola nodded and for the rest of their appointment George remained silent. Even though she wanted to jump in and say what was on her mind, she recognized that she needed to respect Nola's wishes. Later, she would apologize for her behavior and give Nola the chance to talk about how she felt. She made a mental note that when they were alone again, she would listen empathetically and try not to insert herself into the situation by trying to fix everything. The doula was right, it was a stressful time, and to be a supportive wife she would need to take a step back and not act as though she knew it all.

Chapter 13

Podcast #13
Conflicts from Not Having Household
Relationship Agreements

"So often couples complain that they end up having conflicts over "little things" that seem relatively unimportant compared to much bigger issues in life and the relationship. But it is these every day little disagreements that add up and can foster deeper feelings of resentment.

In fact, "relationship agreements" need to happen around a whole host of issues around the house. For example, how clean should the kitchen be kept: are a few crumbs on the counter top okay or should it be completely wiped up after every use? What do you do with the dishes that you've used, do you rinse them, scrape the food off and run it through the garbage disposal, then put it in the dishwasher? Or do you just leave those dishes on the countertop to deal with later?

Here are some other common ones: clutter on the countertops, how clean does the bathroom need to be kept, what temperature do we keep the thermostat on, how do you interrupt one another when you're on the computer or watching a TV show? Each of these and numerous other issues all need to be pre-discussed by every couple in order to avoid the inevitable conflicts that will happen if both are not on the exact same page with the same expectations. Let's talk further about

what needs to happen for a couple to arrive at a "relationship agreement!"

"This seems so silly," Daniel said. "But we've been fighting about the dishwasher lately."

Heather laughed then added, "Yes, but I said if that's all we're fighting about these days then that's a good thing."

The Greens sat in a relaxed position on Dr. Riley's couch. They were back for their weekly session and there hadn't been much going on in their relationship, except for what seemed like petty arguments.

"These little things are valid points to discuss," Dr. Riley said. Though seemingly small, Dr. Riley knew that household matters were important topics for couples to spend time discussing. "These kinds of disagreements may seem trivial when compared to bigger relationship matters, but left unchecked, they can fuel resentment," Dr. Riley added.

"I hear that. It just feels so odd that the thing that really annoys me lately is that she doesn't put the silverware in the dishwasher the proper way," Daniel said with a smile.

"There is no proper way," Heather argued. "They go in the dishwasher and they get clean. That's why we bought the thing. So, I didn't have to think about it."

"But there is a proper way," Daniel argued. "You put one fork prong side down and the next prong side up. Same with all the others. You alternate. That's how it's done."

"Okay, but I don't always do that, and the utensils are usually still clean," Heather sighed.

"Usually is the operative word here," Daniel said as he turned to Dr. Riley for advice.

"Do you want to fix this?" Dr. Riley asked.

"Yes," Daniel said. Heather nodded in concurrence.

"Conflict easily arises out of not having household relationship agreements," Dr. Riley began. "So, you need to talk through these things. In this case, it seems pretty clear that Daniel likes the dishwasher to be loaded in a certain way."

"I do have an order to it," Daniel asserted.

"And I don't think it matters one bit," Heather added with a shrug of her shoulders.

"Great," Dr. Riley said. "So, here's the best way to approach these conflicts regarding household preferences. First, always remember our very different way of approaching romantic love here. It is based on altruistic, unselfish love. Don't fall victim to society's 'me-oriented' self-centered way of looking at love which is so overly concerned with 'not changing oneself.'"

Heather and Daniel both took this in and nodded to assure Dr. Riley they had heard him. He then continued on.

"Differences often occur between partners because one has a higher need for personal order, cleanliness, or organization compared to the other regarding a given domestic issue. And that lack of order/cleanliness causes that partner to be bothered or even anxious in their own home. Typically the other partner is unperturbed and not motivated to change. This causes continued friction. So I recommend something radically different. Don't look at this as being some kind of 'control issue' rather look at it compassionately with altruistic love. Think to yourself: which of us has the need for greater cleanliness, order, organization, or better advanced planning? And if it bothers them in some significant way, more than it does me, then let me do it in exactly the way they prefer out of unselfish love. Let me do it as an active expression of unselfish love for them."

Dr. Riley took a deep breath then finished, "Now that is a beautiful and very different way of being in a relationship that spreads an aura of unselfish loving to everyday life. Don't you think?"

"Definitely," Daniel said.

"Of course," Heather said then continued. "But could you break it down for our relationship?"

"Well, when it comes to loading the dishwasher, Heather, you could choose to load it in the way Daniel prefers out of altruistic love. Because my guess is, there are instances where you feel like there's a certain way to do things and Daniel probably doesn't."

"Uh, yeah. It's called the kitchen," Heather began "To me, what good is perfectly cleaned silverware when the whole rest of the room is a disaster."

"Can you clarify?" Dr. Riley asked.

"Yes. I hate when he cleans the pots and pans and decides to dry them by placing them on the stove top," Heather replied.

"I don't see the big deal," Daniel said. "There's more space. There's plenty of airflow because of the grills over the gas burners and that space is clean."

"That space is clean because I clean it," Heather said then turned to Dr. Riley to explain. "We have a stainless-steel stovetop. When he puts the dishes up there the water drips down, creates water spots and then those spots get gunk on them and somehow our little pet chihuahua's hair ends up stuck on those spots too. It's gross."

"It's not that bad," Daniel said.

"Okay, it's not terrible," Heather replied. "But it's annoying. I spend all that time scrubbing the stove and then I have to do it over every time you wash the dishes. All you'd have to do is dry the pots on a towel and there'd be nothing to talk about."

Dr. Riley looked to Daniel. "Can you see her frustration?"

Daniel nodded. "I get it now. We both have things we like done in specific ways."

"Exactly. And instead of getting into a disagreement about them. You could easily talk through your preferences. We're all human and we have certain things we like done in certain ways. That doesn't mean we can't find a place of mutual agreement."

"I agree," Heather said. "I don't really care about the dishwasher, but if Daniel does then I can make an effort to do things his way."

Daniel smiled, understanding how this whole thing worked. "And I can dry the pots and pans with a towel or buy a drying rack for the side of the sink so that I don't place them on the stove and create more work for you."

"Thank you," Heather said. "I would really appreciate that."

"Well, that was an easy fix," Daniel said. "Do we get our session at half price today?"

Dr. Riley laughed. "No. But I'm happy to see the progress you two are making. I really feel like in a session or two you guys might be ready to go out on your own."

"That sounds scary," Daniel said.

"Nothing we can't handle," Heather said as she reached over and gave Daniel's thigh a gentle squeeze.

Dr. Riley smiled. He was pleased at how much progress the Greens had made over the last few months and he was glad to see them in such good spirits.

"I look forward to our next session," Dr. Riley said as the Greens got up to leave.

"Us too," Daniel replied as they exited the office.

~~~

"You have to talk to your sister," Pilar said. "We're going to freeze to death."

"Don't you think you're being a little dramatic?" Kevin asked as he sat down in the chair next to the bed in their room.

"You're wearing a beanie inside the house," Pilar pointed out.

Kevin sighed. "It's my hipster look."

"I know you're not trying to be stylish," Pilar said. "You only wore that hat in D.C. when the first snow hit the streets. You're now wearing it in the house and there's a heat wave outside."

"Fine," Kevin relented. "I'll go talk to her. But if I don't come back alive it's your fault."

Over the last week, Nola had become pretty on edge. George had told him that it was because she was incredibly uncomfortable at this stage in her pregnancy and she was ready for the baby to be here, so Kevin had cut her some slack. Even so, it was unbearably cold in the house and it was probably time to say something. However, he was hesitating because he never knew what kind of mood his sister would be in these days.

"You'll be fine. She's your sister not a demon," Pilar said.

"Do you want to go up there?" Kevin asked as he pointed to the ceiling.

"Oh. No way," Pilar replied. She'd been tip toeing around Nola all week as well.

"All right. I'll go. Meet in the kitchen in ten? We can grab some lunch and then head out on a hike?"

Pilar nodded. It was Saturday and they had both decided to take some time off from their studies to enjoy the fresh Minnesota air. For October it had been unusually warm, and they wanted to take advantage of the good weather.

~~~

Upstairs, Kevin found Nola lying on her bed wearing a tank top and a loose pair of shorts. Even though it was cold in her room, she had the fan blowing on her. Next to her was a glass of ice water.

"Knock, knock," Kevin said as he stood next to her bed.

Nola opened her eyes. "You know you're actually supposed to knock before you enter, not say it once you're already in here," she said.

"It's good to see you too," Kevin replied. "Where's George?"

"At work. What's up?" Nola asked as she propped herself up in bed and took in the sight of Kevin. "And what's with the hat?"

"Um, not much," Kevin started. "Just thought I'd come in and check on you. Also, did you know that your AC system is connected to downstairs?"

"It feels good, doesn't it?" Nola smiled.

"Actually, it's a lot colder down there," Kevin said. "I was going to see if you could turn it down a bit."

"I'm about ready to burst, Kevin. There's an alien inside me bouncing on my bladder and I feel like I'm in Palm Springs in the middle of summer," Nola sighed.

"Well, when you put it that way, that sounds awful," Kevin said. "I'm sorry I asked."

"I wish I could just go on vacation and return when the baby was here," Nola smiled as she remembered the first vacation she and George took together as a couple. They rented a house in the Movie Colony area of Palm Springs where it was rumored Dean Martin had once spent his days off relaxing by the pool. She really wished she could escape there now. But right now, her brother was hovering over her.

"Did Pilar send you up here?" Nola asked. Kevin nodded. "There're some extra blankets in the closet if you want to take them," Nola said. "I'm sorry. I wish I could help but I don't see how I'm going to budge on this one."

Kevin thought about saying more, negotiating with Nola and coming to a good compromise. But seeing how uncomfortable Nola looked he couldn't bring himself to do it.

"It's understandable," Kevin said. "I'll handle Pilar. Don't worry about it."

~~~

A few minutes later, Kevin walked into the kitchen carrying a stack of warm winter blankets. Pilar was sitting at the island with Kulap.

"What's that?" Pilar asked as she turned to Kevin.

"Nola's not budging on the AC," he said as he put the blankets down on an empty chair.

"So, we just bundle up, then?" Pilar asked with a sigh.

"You should see her. She looks miserable," Kevin replied. "I couldn't say anything."

"Okay," Pilar relented. "I guess we can manage for a few more weeks."

"Technically, I think she could have the baby any day," Kevin said.

"What?" Kulap asked. "She hasn't reached her due day yet. Has she?"

"You're asking me? I don't know, but it's not unheard of to go into labor early is it?" Kevin asked right back.

Kulap shrugged. "Don't look at me. I never had kids. But I have to say, I like having Nola around."

"Really?" Kevin asked.

"Yeah. I was wondering who's been turning the temperature down," Kulap said. "I have to say, it's making me pretty happy." Kulap then turned to Pilar and said, "Don't get old. Hot flashes are the worst."

Kevin gave her a look.

"What?" Kulap asked. "Oh, you thought I was going to say that I really enjoy having all of you living here just for the sake of having our adult children around?"

"Ah, yeah," Kevin smiled but Pilar stayed quiet.

"Don't get me wrong. I love you guys, but you can understand, can't you?" Kulap asked.

"Absolutely," Pilar said thinking about how many disagreements she and Kevin had already gotten into about living at the Riley lake house.

"The good thing about Nola is that your dad's a softie just like you, Kevin. He's not going to be able to tell her what to do either," Kulap said. "And that's good for me."

"How so?" Pilar said.

"Oh, we negotiated the temperature control years ago," Kulap said. "Your dad sleeps hot, so he's allowed to turn the thermostat down at night. During the day I get hot, so I'm allowed to keep it temperate. But your sister's taken temperate to a new level. One that if I did it, would definitely push some boundaries. Or call for a renegotiation. So, Nola being in charge is great."

"You guys really negotiate all of this stuff?" Kevin asked.

"Of course, they do," Pilar said. "Didn't you listen to the podcast this week?"

"I did. But I always thought that when he talks about his marriage, he exaggerates a bit just to prove a point," Kevin said as he sat down at the kitchen table.

"No. We really do follow your dad's principles," Kulap said just as Dr. Steve entered the room.

"Are you telling them all the secrets to our happy marriage?" Dr. Steve asked as he gave Kulap a kiss on the cheek.

"Not all of them," Kulap said with a flirtatious flick of her hair.

"Good," Dr. Steve said. "So, what's happening in here?"

"Just a negotiation of the family AC trust," Kulap said in a matter of fact tone.

"I noticed it's been cold around here lately," Dr. Steve said.

"We've negotiated that none of us here are going to touch it," Pilar said. "Instead, we'll all be making adjustments for the next few weeks."

"Ah, a pregnancy situation?" Dr. Steve asked as he finally understood. Everyone nodded. "I see. Then I'll happily follow along with this family plan."

"Good," Kulap said with a wink to Pilar.

Just then Dr. Steve heard the roar of Chet's boat approaching the dock outside. The sound gave Dr. Steve an idea.

"Where's Nola now?" Dr. Steve asked.

"In her room," Kevin said.

"You think she'd want some fresh air?" Dr. Steve continued. Everyone shrugged, because no one knew what Nola wanted at this point, but Kulap finally spoke up.

"If the temp outside has gone down, I don't see why she wouldn't want to come out," Kulap said. "Why do you ask?"

"Chet owes me a ride. I thought you'd all want to come," Dr. Steve said.

"That sounds fun," Pilar said. "I owe Chet some champagne from that day we moved in. Is it cool to bring a bottle?"

"Sure," Dr. Steve said.

Pilar grabbed a bottle of champagne from the small wine fridge in the Riley dining room while Dr. Steve went and retrieved Nola. She was reluctant to leave her bed at first, but Dr. Steve convinced her that it would be good for her to get out.

"What about George?" Nola asked.

"We'll be back before she's home from work," Dr. Steve said.

Nola couldn't argue with this and thought a ride on the lake would be a nice distraction from the discomfort she was currently feeling in her body. The two walked through the kitchen and gathered the rest of the crew. Together, the Riley family made their way to the water.

Down at the dock, Chet greeted them with a smile.

"Didn't know the whole clan was coming," Chet said. "But it's good to see you guys."

"I brought champagne," Pilar said holding up the bottle.

"In that case, it's great to see you all," Chet said as he helped each of the women onto the boat and asked Dr. Steve and Kevin to help untie the lines and push them off from the dock.

They sped through the open water, passing other boats and homes where people waved from their docks. It was a perfect fall afternoon even though it was nearly eighty degrees. However, the temperature had dropped as the sun had begun to set and there was a cool breeze in the air.

Chet drove them to one of the secluded coves along the lake and dropped anchor. The large maple trees on the shore cast a shadow on the water placing them out of the direct sunlight so they could relax in the quiet of nature.

"Anyone want to take a swim?" Chet asked.

Everyone shook their head no. Although it had been an incredibly hot day, the water was anything but warm.

For the next hour, the Riley family enjoyed each other's company. Kevin and Pilar sat on the bow of the boat with Chet sipping champagne while Kulap and Dr. Steve sat with Nola on the bench seats at the back of the boat snacking on cheese and crackers.

"I feel like I should apologize," Nola said.

"For what?" Dr. Steve asked.

Kulap gave him a playful slap on the knee. "Let her talk," Kulap said.

"You guys have been so good to me and George and I know it hasn't been easy on you," Nola said. "But living here has really helped us."

"Well, that just made your day didn't it?" Kulap said as she turned to Dr. Steve.

Dr. Steve smiled and nodded.

"What was the apology for then?" Kulap asked.

"Oh, I know I've kind of been in my own world lately with the baby coming and I've probably been a little selfish," Nola said.

"How so?" Kulap asked.

"You know, I know it's cold in the house and that'll eventually change," Nola replied in reference to the AC situation. "But also, I know that if we're going to live here for the next year…"

"The next year?" Kulap gasped. She hadn't been expecting them to stay that long. Nola paused and looked at her dad.

"It's okay, Nola, she's just kidding," Dr. Steve said with a glance to Kulap indicating that she should listen instead of interjecting.

"I know that if we're staying then we need to set some house rules," Nola said.

"Not necessarily rules," Dr. Steve said.

"No. I know. They're household agreements," Nola replied.

"I'm glad to hear you've been paying attention," Dr. Steve said.

"Oh, I have, but would you mind if we put them off for a little while longer? At least, until this baby arrives," Nola said.

"And when is that again?" Kulap asked.

"A couple weeks," Nola replied. "Hopefully sooner."

Before Kulap could say anymore, Chet shouted from the front of the boat. "Hey! You all want to have some fun or are you just going to keep having serious conversations back there."

"We're ready for some fun," Kulap said as she stood up from her seat and walked to the middle of the boat where Chet was fumbling with the radio. He turned up the volume on a great song that made everyone want to dance. They started to get in a groove.

Everyone was laughing and smiling and enjoying one another's company that they failed to notice the boat was drifting. The anchor had slipped, and they were no longer tied to a steady spot in the lake. Instead, they were slowly moving towards shore.

No one noticed until there was a large crack and a huge thud.

"That did not sound normal," Pilar stated as she grabbed onto Kevin's arm to steady herself.

"It's fine," Chet said as he turned down the volume on the radio. "Happens all the time."

"Are you sure?" Kevin asked as he peered over the side of the boat. "Because that looks like a pretty big scratch and a large pile of rocks."

"It's no big deal," Chet said as he stood at the helm and turned the key in the engine. The engine started without a problem however water spewed everywhere.

"Arghh!" Kulap and Nola shouted as they stepped away from the back of the boat to avoid the waterspout that was coming from the engine area.

"Did you forget to drop the motor?" Kevin asked.

"No," Chet said. "It's dropped."

"Then we're on land, or something," Kevin replied as he looked off the back of the boat and saw that the propellers weren't fully submerged.

Chet turned the key the other direction and the motor stopped. He and Kevin and Dr. Steve inspected the area. They were indeed perched atop a pile of rocks.

"I think we might have to get out and push," Dr. Steve announced.

"None of us women are doing that," Kulap said.

"I don't mind," Pilar said. "I used to lifeguard. I have no problem getting in."

"The water's freezing," Kevin said. "You hate the cold."

"The water's not freezing," Chet said with a gasp. "The water's coming into our boat!"

"No, it's not!" Nola exclaimed as she looked down at the space around her with her eyes wide open. "That's my water."

"What?" Chet asked.

"I think I'm about to have a baby," Nola said.

"Out here?" Kulap exclaimed.

"I hope not," Nola said. "But we should get going."

Everyone started to panic and rush around the boat.

"I'm trying the engine again," Chet said.

"No," Dr. Steve said. "Use this oar to push us off the rock."

"That's not going to work," Kulap added. "Someone has to go in."

Chet then turned around to Kevin and said, "Good luck."

Kevin pulled off his shirt and jumped into the water. Pilar helped Nola relax into the front seat that wrapped around the bow of the boat.

"Holy--!," Kevin shouted from the water as he came up for air. "That's cold."

"Now you know how I've been feeling inside the house," Pilar shouted back.

"That's nothing compared to this," Kevin yelled.

"You guys," Nola shouted at them all. "Can we discuss temperature differences of the water and house later? I need to get back on land." Nola clasped her stomach. The contractions were setting in. "Like now!"

Everyone got down to business. The baby was coming, they were stuck out at sea and it felt chaotic. No amount of preparation or communication could've readied them for this moment. But they were working together as a family with the help of Chet to get back on land and straight to the hospital.

After a twenty-minute struggle, Chet, Dr. Steve and Kevin managed to free the boat from the rocks. Once they got back to the dock, Kevin and Chet put their arms around Nola and helped her walk to the driveway. Nola's contractions were still far enough apart that they still had time to get to the hospital, yet the pain was intensifying. Without a second thought, the Rileys loaded into Dr. Steve's car. Chet remained behind.

"Send me updates," Chet shouted after them with a wave as they sped off to the hospital.

Nola sat in the backseat leaning against the door with her legs resting on top of Kulap and Pilar's laps. Pilar gently rubbed Nola's ankles as Kulap sat still in the middle seat. Kulap was concentrating on maintaining a calm, even breath. *Inhale, two, three, four. Exhale, two, three, four.* She kept repeating this mantra over and over to herself. Her hope was that her breath rhythm would be noticeable, and Nola would follow suit. Though she'd had little experience with the birth process, she knew enough to know that maintaining a sense of calm would help everyone.

As the car turned the corner, Kevin turned the volume up on the radio. Jazz played over the speakers.

"Can you turn it down?" Nola asked with an exasperated voice. Nola was freaking out and the dissonant melodies of the trumpet and saxophone lines were making her more stressed. She felt like there were a million things she was supposed to do in the moment, like she had forgotten something important for the birth. "Oh god, did someone call George?"

Kulap nodded. "I did. She's meeting us there," she said.

"Thank you," Nola sighed then winced at the pain of the start of another contraction.

"Who's gonna call the baby's daddy?" Kevin asked with a glance at Pilar.

"You can give me the number and I'll call him for you," Pilar said as she eagerly pulled out her cell phone.

"Not a chance you two," Nola replied as she realized what they were doing. "George will handle it."

Pilar gave Kevin a look like, *we almost had it.*

Just then another wave of contractions came over Nola. "Come on, Dad, you got to go faster," Nola said with a look into the rearview mirror. Dr. Steve knew that look. It was the look that said, I'm serious.

"Okay, I'm just concentrating on getting us there safely," Dr. Steve said as he focused on the wheel and the road ahead.

"I don't care," Nola screamed out in pain. "This baby's coming."

Dr. Steve pressed the gas a little harder. Even though the drive felt stressful, he couldn't help but be excited. He was about to become a grandfather. His whole world was going to change, and he knew it was only going to get better. Despite the chaos that had ensued throughout the last few months having his kids and their spouses living with him, there was nothing better than having family close by, even if they were in all the spare rooms or the backseat about to give birth.

Chapter 14

Podcast #14
Conflicts from Not Making
Parenting Agreements

"There is one type of relationship agreement that deserves special attention, namely 'parenting agreements.' One common source of conflict that can become quite serious in a relationship involves differences in parenting approach. Typically, one parent is 'harder' while the other is 'softer.'

There are a variety of complaints such as: 'you let them get away with everything and there are no consequences, you are too harsh and yell at them too much, you are too easy on them, you make threats but never act on them, etc.' When one partner feels their ideas and wishes about parenting suggestions are not being heard or dismissed, resentment can build up that has the potential for becoming quite damaging to the relationship.

Both parents must pay particular attention to listening to the needs of one another regarding their parenting approach and try to come to a nice balance incorporating both partners' wishes. Let's explore how to do this and I'll share my approach of The High Respect Choice Method of Parenting which will make both parents happy whether they are 'harder' or 'softer.'"

"Awwww… is that him?" Heather gushed as she entered Dr. Riley's office and spotted a newly framed photo on his desk.

Dr. Riley smiled. "That's him," he said. "Baby Nicholas."

"Are you loving being a grandpa?" Heather asked.

"I am," Dr. Riley replied. "It's pretty incredible."

"One day we'll be there too," Daniel said as he looked wistfully at the photo. Then he quipped, "If we can survive the teenage years."

Heather ignored Daniel's comment and continued gushing. "He's too cute," she said. "Almost makes me want to have another." She turned to face Daniel with a pouty face. "Don't you miss that baby phase?"

Daniel thought for a moment then replied, "Actually, I kind of do. Despite the no sleep thing, they're really great when they're that little." Daniel sunk into the couch with a sigh.

"Yeah. They are," Heather said then thought about her own kids and turned to Dr. Riley to explain. "Our daughter's going through a phase. She's twelve going on twenty."

Dr. Riley took his seat across from Daniel and Heather. He could tell they were ready to start their session and dig into their current issues.

"She used to be so sweet," Daniel said, "But now, I feel like she wants nothing to do with us. Which I get. We were all embarrassed of our parents at some point. But when I was that young, it was not an excuse to miss out on family time."

"And that's our problem," Heather began. "Because I don't really see the issue of her wanting to do her own thing. I think it's good for girls to learn how to assert their independence."

"I don't disagree with that fact," Daniel replied. "I just don't think she can skip out on an afternoon with us and her brother because she thinks something's childish."

Dr. Riley looked at Heather to further the story.

"We went apple picking on Sunday and she said she didn't want to come. She said that it was for little kids and she'd rather stay home," Heather explained. "I kind of understood, so I gave her permission to stay back."

Daniel shook his head in disagreement. He was clearly annoyed by what had transpired. Dr. Riley took note. "So, this upset you?" Dr. Riley asked Daniel.

"Yes, because we had agreed that family time was important to us," Daniel stated. "That has always been part of our relationship since before the kids were born."

From the day he and Heather started talking about marriage, Daniel had been insistent about family time. His own family wasn't close. His dad worked too much and his mom never forced the issue. Because of his parents' dynamic he always felt like he'd missed out on an important part of growing up. He didn't want that for his kids.

"He's right," Heather said. "Family time has always been important to both of us. But I think there needs to be some wiggle room here. Especially now that the kids are getting older."

"And I think it's non-negotiable," Daniel replied. "The kids still need rules, and before one of us goes and changes them we need to discuss it first." Daniel crossed his arms across his chest. Heather noticed the change in his demeanor, and she understood.

"So that's why you're upset," she said. "This isn't about family time, it's more about the fact that I changed the rules and let her stay home?"

"Yes," Daniel said.

"Well, you could've just said that," Heather replied.

"Yeah, but I thought you would understand," Daniel said. "I didn't think I had to spell it out."

Heather took a deep breath then looked at Dr. Riley. She knew what had gone wrong. "I guess this comes back to clarifying and coaching each other," she said.

"Yes. That would help," Dr. Riley replied. "In the same way that you worked on household agreements last week, you need to do that here."

"So, my kid is like the dishwasher now?" Daniel laughed.

"Not quite," Dr. Riley said. "I would say that these parenting agreements have a little more weight. However, just like with household agreements if you don't discuss them and come to a mutual place of understanding you will build resentment."

"I can see that," Heather said. "So, what do we do?"

"That's up to you two to find a way that works with both of your parenting styles," Dr. Riley replied.

Heather and Daniel each thought about different solutions then Heather spoke first. "What if you and I came to an agreement that family time is non-negotiable. I'll promise not to let her stay home, however I think we need to change the way family time works a little bit."

"I'm open to suggestions," Daniel said.

"We've always made our activities about what we thought was best for the family. But the kids are older now and have ideas too. What if we asked for the kids to give us suggestions on what they want to do," Heather presented.

Daniel thought about this for a moment then replied, "I think that's a great idea. It'll make them feel more involved."

"Exactly. So, we agree?" Heather asked. "We'll keep Sunday afternoons as family time, but we'll alternate who chooses what we do."

"Yes. I agree," Daniel said. He felt good about this plan and he was pleased that they had come up with it together.

"This is a great approach," Dr. Riley said. "Showing your kids that you value their ideas will make them feel respected."

"And that's exactly what we want," Daniel said. "That's one of the things we really loved about your parenting approach in the last podcast."

"Remember," Dr. Riley began, "these kinds of issues will come up again but if you can come back to this calm place and come to an agreement together, I think it'll stay pretty easy."

"I hope so," Heather said. "If not, we know where to find you."

"We're not leaving him already, are we?" Daniel asked.

"No. You have one more session scheduled for next week," Dr. Riley replied.

"Good," Daniel said. Even though they had learned an incredible amount from Dr. Riley, Daniel wasn't quite ready to leave yet.

"Thank you for another good session," Heather said as she gathered her belongings. "Now you go home and get some sleep. Before that baby runs you wild."

~~~

There was no sleep in the immediate future for Dr. Riley, he had more work to do that day. He was giving a seminar on parenting.

Dr. Riley had briefly touched on his High Respect Choice Method for Parenting in the podcast, but this was a seminar to go deeper. After receiving so many emails and comments from parents on the episode wanting to know more and thanking Dr. Riley for sharing his method, Ryan, Dr. Riley's producer, saw an opportunity to expand Dr. Riley's reach. This seemed like a natural and organic first step to take.

Dr. Riley met Ryan at Macalester University. Ryan had rented a lecture room for Dr. Riley to give his talk. The presentation section of the seminar was purposely kept short so that Dr. Riley could open up the floor to questions.

When his speaking portion was over, he asked the audience if anyone wanted to share their recent parenting successes or failures and talk through them.

One of the audience members raised their hand to volunteer her situation. She told the story of her and her husband and their approach to their kids' school work. "He thinks I'm too soft, but I think he's too hard on them," she said.

"Can you give me an example?" Dr. Riley prompted her.

"Sure, our oldest son is thirteen. He does really well when he applies himself, but currently he's more interested in making short videos for his YouTube channel than studying algebra. My husband thinks this is the worst thing in the world. I think it's incredible how creative my son is. I, personally, don't care if he brings home a B if it means he's focused on something he loves. My husband, however, doesn't think this is an option. To him, school is the end all be all, and if my son isn't focused on school, he's too tough and too harsh about it with him. Me? I'm the opposite. I think that kids have more choices for the future these days and I don't want to discourage my son from exploring that."

Dr. Riley took in the woman's story and thought about the best approach. "It sounds like you both want the best for your kid, but you disagree about what the best is. Your husband sees good grades as a means to future success, and you think success can come from following your passion."

"Exactly. I don't believe college is the same guarantor of success that it used to be. And I don't want my kid to be in debt just for a piece of paper."

"That's a valid point. But he still needs to graduate high school, right?" Dr. Riley asked.

"Of course," the mom said.

"And he'll be in a better spot to do whatever he wants to do if he gets good grades now, correct?" Dr. Riley prompted.

"Yes. I believe there are many important lessons to be learned in school at this age," the mom said.

"Great, so let me explain my approach," Dr. Riley began. "It starts with coming to a specific agreement with your husband. In your case, it's probably agreeing that your son should get good grades and finish high school but also not stop following his dreams."

"Okay? But how does that encourage my son to do these things?" the mom asked.

"This is where the "choice method" comes into play," Dr. Riley began. "With the choice method, you say to your son "you have a choice of either doing your homework or losing the privileges of your camera and the internet." I'm assuming he needs these two things for his YouTube?" The mom nodded. "Great. So, if he completes his homework and does his best to study and get the good grades he is capable of then he has full rein to make as many videos as he wants. The way to communicate this to him is to do so in a completely respectful way with a tone of voice that has not even a hint of any authoritarian, angry, irritated, or impatient tone. You just nicely say that he has a choice. He can put forth this effort to be responsible in school which is so important to success in life and have the privilege of the camera and internet, or he can choose to lose that privilege."

The mom nodded in understanding.

Dr. Riley continued on, "When you present this to your son, it's important that you start by saying that you and your husband have made the decision to not ever yell or get upset with him. You will just treat him respectfully and simply give him the "choice" between doing his responsibility or losing his privileges."

"That sounds great, but what do I tell my husband who's a bit more demanding? If it were up to him, he'd say do the homework or get nothing," the woman asked.

"That's a good point to bring up," Dr. Riley replied. "It may be difficult for parents to change their style of getting upset with their children. But telling a kid in a punishing tone: "if you don't do this, then this is going happen to you!" is not an example of the High Respect Choice Method, rather it is an authoritarian approach which the child will be even more likely to react to and behave just the opposite to defy you. Or they may do what you ask but then feel inner resentment about that authoritarian tone which can build up over time. And this can contribute to more distance in the relationship."

"And this works every time?" the mom asked.

"You might need to adjust a few things. The key to a consequence is that it's not so severe that it destroys the motivation but that it's strong enough for them that they will change their behavior. The important thing to remember as parents though is to remain calm and give the child the choice with a tone of complete respect so that there will be nothing for the child to react to and rebel against."

The woman sat silent to take it all in, which gave Dr. Riley a moment to look out into the audience. He noticed a lot of people nodding in agreement to his plan, but a few puzzled looks as well. He continued on to explain further, "As a parent, you need to remember to take the attitude that it's a choice to make and that's okay. The child is making that choice and you go along with it. If the child complains, you just say in a compassionate tone of voice, 'I'm so sorry you chose to lose X instead of doing A, B, or C, especially when X is so important to you.' This puts the responsibility on the child and allows you as parents to remain neutral so that neither parent has to take the role of being too hard or too soft." Dr. Riley paused and let all of the information sink in. Then he added, "Oh, and you're right in that you and your husband have to be 100% on the same page to do this. Most men who tend to be too "hard" on their kids are relieved to hear that there will finally be consistent consequences." He then looked at the mom and asked, "Does that help?"

"Yes. Thank you," the mom said.

"You're welcome," Dr Riley said as he looked at his watch. Time was just about up. "Thank you all for coming here today. It has been my pleasure."

The audience clapped as Dr. Riley graciously nodded his head. He then looked to Ryan who was sitting in the first row giving him a thumbs up. Dr. Riley took this as a sign that the seminar was a success and was happy to be done with his day so that he could return to home to his family.

~~~

Dr. Steve arrived at the lake house later that night to find Kulap, Nola and George fast asleep in the living room. If he didn't know better, he'd have thought they'd pulled an all-nighter, partying into the early hours of the morning. But since the birth of the baby, hardly anyone had gotten a full nights' rest. He tiptoed into the room and picked up the baby monitor, then silently walked into the sitting room that overlooked the lake.

He sat down in his favorite leather chair and propped his feet up on the ottoman. He then placed the monitor on the armrest and watched as baby Nicholas slept soundly.

The house was incredibly quiet. In fact, it hadn't been this quiet since the night Dr. Steve and Kulap camped out in this very room when they purchased the house. Dr. Steve took a moment to take it all in. He daydreamed about the last few months – how much they'd been through as a family. Despite the many adjustments that had been made, he really did enjoy having everyone nearby, especially now that the baby had arrived.

Dr. Steve's thoughts were interrupted by a small movement out of the corner of his eye. He looked over at the monitor. The baby was stirring and beginning to open his eyes. Dr. Steve quietly stood up and rushed to Nola and George's room. Luckily, he arrived at the bassinet just as the baby was about to start wailing. Dr. Steve picked him up and cradled him across his chest to soothe him.

Nicholas cooed in the soft way that babies do, and Dr. Steve breathed in the fresh smell of his skin. It was amazing to be here in this moment nearly thirty years after his own children were born. He thought about life and how things always come full circle. He paused in that moment to meditate on the beauty of it all. When the baby started to fuss, Dr. Steve tried to soothe Nicholas by bending his knees in a smooth rhythm to bounce the baby, but he knew Nicholas had to be hungry. He made his way into the kitchen and opened the fridge. He found several bags of pumped breast milk and was about to heat one up when he noticed a container of formula on the counter. Now he was stumped.

What was he supposed to feed the baby? Last time, Nola took him and the time before that George fed him a bottle. But what was in the bottle? Was there a new protocol? If there was anything Dr. Steve remembered about newborns, it was that everything was a constant experiment—always changing.

Luckily, just as panic was setting in, George walked into the room.

"He's up?" she said as she wiped her groggy eyes.

"I didn't want to wake you," Dr. Steve said. "You all looked so peaceful when I got home so I took his monitor."

"Thank you," George said. "I needed the extra rest. Nola's still out."

"I think he's hungry," Dr. Steve said.

George walked over to Dr. Steve and the baby and took a sniff of his behind. "He also needs a diaper change," she said in a matter of fact manner.

Dr. Steve held the baby up and realized George was right. "I am definitely out of practice," he said. "I was so worried about what to feed him that I didn't even think about his diaper."

"It's no problem," George replied. "You've been an incredible help. Why don't I go change him and you fix a bottle?"

"Of what?" Dr. Steve asked.

"Whiskey," George said with a smile. "And he likes it neat."

"So, breast milk?" Dr. Steve guessed.

"Yes," George said as she gently took the baby from Dr. Steve's arms.

"You got it," Dr. Steve said as he made his way to the fridge. While Dr. Steve was preparing the bottle, Nola sauntered in.

"What are you doing?" Nola asked.

"Warming a bottle," Dr. Steve explained.

"With that?" Nola said in a panic. "That's like liquid gold. Do you know how long it took me to make that?"

Dr. Steve hit pause on the warming machine. "I'm sorry, I didn't know. George told me this was fine."

"I mean it kind of is, but I was hoping to sleep through the night tonight and George was going to wake up with him at two. That bottle was supposed to be for her to feed him," Nola explained.

"I'm so sorry," Dr. Steve said.

"It's okay," Nola replied. She was too tired to worry any further or talk through anything. She knew that eventually they would get the hang of the parenting and grandparenting routine and they'd divvy up the bathing, cleaning clothes, feeding, and changing in a way that made sense for everyone. They would have a conversation to be clear on how it would all work, until then, they would keep moving forward.

Just then George returned with a happy baby. Nola looked to her dad. "I guess it's dinner time. Go ahead," she said as she handed the precious bottle to Dr. Steve.

Dr. Steve took Nicholas and made his way back to his chair where he watched as the baby drank then drifted in and out of sleep. Nola smiled at the sight and snuggled in to the chair next to them. Seeing her baby in her dad's arms made her feel safe and in good hands. She was grateful to have her entire family's support. That night she climbed into bed feeling content.

Later, however, at two am, Nola, though completely exhausted, was wide awake. Her mind spun with thoughts of parenthood.

Was she doing everything correctly? Was she already messing him up for life? Would there be something she did today that would send him to therapy fifteen years from now? She was so overwhelmed she woke George.

"What's wrong? Is he okay? Are you okay?" George asked as she turned over in bed.

"I'm fine," Nola whimpered. "I'm just in pain, exhausted and I can't believe we're doing this."

"Doing what?" George asked.

"Raising a baby," Nola cried.

"Nola, you knew this was happening over ten months ago," George said.

"I know. And I know it's going to be fine. But it's so much," Nola whimpered. George put her hand on Nola's shoulder and gently rubbed her.

"We'll get through it," George said trying to calm her.

"But will we?" Nola asked with genuine concern.

"Yes, we will. What makes you think we won't?" George asked.

"I don't know. There's so much to think about now. Like who's going to be the disciplinarian—you or me?" Nola asked.

"Probably you," George laughed.

"It's not funny," Nola said.

"I know. But he's nine pounds," George said looking over at their sleeping baby. "It's hard to imagine yelling at him for anything right now."

"See, that's my point, are we both going to be too easy, love him too much, and let him get away with everything? Then he turns into a delinquent, drug taking slacker who never achieves anything in life. Maybe he ends up in jail. And it'll all be our fault!" Nola was spiraling.

"Don't worry," George said. "You've forgotten, we already have this one nipped in the bud."

"We do?" Nola asked confused.

"Absolutely," George reassured her. "Remember how we both heard your dad's podcast on raising kids. We'll follow his way of never yelling at them and showing them complete respect while at the same time holding them totally responsible with consequences "

Nola softened. "We both did love that whole idea of not talking to your kids in an angry or impatient way. And how he pointed out that it's not ok to talk disrespectfully just because they're children. If we wouldn't talk to a boss or close friend that way, then we shouldn't talk to our kids that way."

"Absolutely," George responded. "You see, we're in complete agreement already. And maybe we don't have to figure this all out right now," George said. "Maybe we can focus on one thing at a time."

Nola took a deep breath. Focusing on one thing sounded like a good idea. "Okay. How?" she asked aloud. George thought about this for a moment.

"Let's just agree to work on keeping him alive," George said.

"Was there any moment where that wasn't an option?" Nola gasped.

"Of course not," George said. "But we're new to this. If we look at the big picture, our greatest job is to care for him and love him. And if that's all we have to worry about then I think we're going to be amazing parents."

Nola took a deep breath and nodded in agreement.

"I think we should enjoy each day," George said. "He's going to grow up fast and if we spend all our time worrying, we're going to miss it."

Nola breathed another deep breath and this time sighed it out. "You're right," she said then reached over and interlaced her fingers in George's. It was moments like this that made her remember why she fell in love with George in the first place. Sure, George hadn't always been the most reliable, but her carefree laid-back attitude also balanced out Nola's own need to control everything. George was right, they were going to be good parents. In fact, they already were. She leaned out of bed and over the bassinet and gently kissed the top of Nicholas' head.

Then George kissed Nola's forehead. They both smiled. They were going to be okay.

Chapter 15

Podcast #15
Love Building Skills: Positives, Love
Affirmations, and Flirting

"I hear from couples all the time who say, 'I know we should be more loving and more romantic with one another, however we just don't have the time or energy.' And they ask me what they can do to create a more passionate relationship.

My response is that there are clearly defined best practices to deepen the emotional love bond. 'Yes, there are skills to intensify positive feelings of fondness and love.' Sustaining wonderful feelings of love in a relationship won't just happen by itself.

You can decide to proactively say and do those things in a relationship to create positive energy and feelings, or you can sit back and comfortably cruise. The question you have to ask yourself is, 'do I want more in my relationship?' If the answer is yes, then consider the possibility that you can consciously create deeper feelings of love.

There are Four Best Practices for Sustaining Passion and Romance

    1) Positives: Compliments and Appreciation

    2) Love Affirmations

    3) Loving Acts of Kindness

    4) Romantic Flirting"

The Greens sat comfortably on Dr. Riley's couch during their final session. They had gone over any questions they had about continuing forward with the process and were just about done.

"I want to leave you with a few little reminders," Dr. Riley said. "These are things you should do daily to continue showing your love for one another."

"I think we can do that," Heather said. Daniel nodded to indicate that he was on board.

"Every day I want you both to think about ways you can point out the positives in each other, give love affirmations, and flirt," Dr. Riley added. "These don't have to be grand gestures or take a ton of time or thought to do, but they will continue to help you stay on this path."

"I like that," Heather replied. "The small things really do make a difference."

"Exactly," Dr. Riley said. "Remembering to leave a short note on the bathroom mirror for one another, or offering to rub the other's back or picking up slack around the house without being asked to do it, shows your commitment to keeping your love alive. You two have come a long way and I want to see you continue growing together."

Over the last few months Dr. Riley had come to appreciate his time with the Greens. Watching them reconnect by learning how to Co-Coach one another in Softly Specific ways, meet each other's Love Needs, identify their Negative Relationship Patterns, address underlying resentment, graciously accept feedback and work through their assumptions of negative intent, had given Dr. Riley a renewed sense of pride in his work. He knew this would always be an ongoing process for the Greens as it is with every couple he works with, but he was content with the progress they'd made. They were happy too.

"Thank you for everything," Daniel said. "I feel like we're supposed to go out and celebrate now," he added. Though there was no true matriculation to couples' therapy, this day felt like a graduation of sorts.

"I have a better idea," Dr. Riley began. "How about we end our session with each of you sharing a positive about the other regarding your work together here."

The Greens agreed this was a good idea.

Dr. Riley directed them to turn and face one another. They looked into one another's eyes, held hands, and each thought about what to say. A couple minutes later, Heather began.

"I appreciate the fact that you trusted me in coming here and really gave it your all," she said. When she had first mentioned therapy, Daniel wasn't against it, but he definitely wasn't completely for it either. However, she had watched him take to it in a way she'd never expected. "I'm impressed with how serious you were about this process. Not just showing up here week after week, but really taking the time to apply everything we learned from Dr. Riley in our day-to-day lives," Heather said.

"I was happy to do it," Daniel said then reached over and held Heather's hand. Now it was his turn.

"I love that even when things got difficult you didn't give up," Daniel said. He knew that there were many times during their Co-Coaching work where Heather became incredibly frustrated with him. "You let me work things out on my own time and I appreciate that," Daniel finished.

Heather smiled. They leaned into one another and embraced. Dr. Riley was pleased with the sight. It was evident that they were going to be just fine and if they weren't, "Remember you can always come back here any time you need. Couples benefit greatly from a few booster sessions if there's any major slipping back," Dr. Riley said.

"You're in my contacts now," Daniel replied.

"Thank you for everything," Heather added.

As Dr. Riley walked the Greens to the door, he felt a sense of accomplishment. Not just for everything the Greens had made their way through, but for everything that had coincided with his time with the Greens. Nola moving back home. George coming with her. The baby. Kevin and Pilar moving into the house as well. Learning to adjust to having everyone home and still honoring his commitment to Kulap and nurturing their relationship. Plus, maintaining his focus on his career through everything. None of it was easy, but all of it was welcome.

He never imagined that his adult children would move back home with him, that he would have a podcast and a growing business, that Kulap would become an integral part of his children's lives, and that being a grandparent would be so fulfilling, yet here he was and he couldn't have been happier.

~~~

That afternoon Dr. Steve met Kulap for a late lunch at their favorite diner. When he entered the establishment, Kulap was already seated at the counter. Her back was turned towards him, her head down as she read over the menu. He walked past the hostess with a nod to say, *I'm meeting someone over there.* Then he snuck up behind Kulap and gently brushed past her—his hip grazing the small of her back.

Kulap instinctively turned to look at the offender, ready to say *excuse me.* But Dr. Steve was quicker.

"I'm so sorry, miss. I didn't mean to bump you," Dr. Steve flirted then eyed the stool next to her. "Is this seat taken?"

"For you?" she asked, eyeing him up and down. "It's empty," Kulap said, playing along.

"Oh good. Because I'm starving," Dr. Steve said.

"Well then, you're in luck. So, am I," Kulap replied with a wink then asked, "Buy me lunch?"

"Absolutely," Dr. Steve said.

After the waitress took their order, they settled in to their seats and relished in the relative quiet moment they were having together.

"Is it weird that I kind of miss the baby's cries?" Kulap asked. "I mean it's only been an hour, but I've never been so obsessed with someone in my life." Despite the fact that Kulap had been reluctant to let the kids live with them long term she couldn't imagine a world where baby Nicholas didn't live there. She loved having him around. Sure, having her own space again would be nice, but the soft sounds of a baby were incredibly calming, and she found it attractive how attentive and helpful Dr. Steve was in caring for him.

"I think it's adorable, that you miss him, Grandma," Dr. Steve said.

"About that, do you think we could ask Nola and George for a better name for me? I just don't feel like a grandmother," Kulap said.

"Sure. I don't see why not," Dr. Steve replied.

"I know I wasn't around when the kids were young, but I can tell you were a great dad," Kulap said.

"Were?" Dr. Steve joked.

"You know what I meant," Kulap said. "It's pretty incredible to see you with him. It's a whole other side I've never witnessed, and I like it," she finished as she leaned over and kissed him.

Dr. Steve kissed her back. He liked it too.

~~~

Meanwhile, across town, Kevin stood next to the car in the campus parking lot. He was waiting for Pilar who was hurriedly approaching.

"Am I late?" Pilar asked as she finally reached him.

"No, you're fine," Kevin said. "I got out early."

"Oh good," Pilar replied as she opened the back door and threw in her bags. "You driving?"

Kevin nodded and got into the driver's seat.

Pilar followed and sat in her spot. She seemed distracted. "I'm sorry," she said. "It's been a hectic day."

"It's okay," Kevin said then went on. "I've got a surprise."

"For me?" Pilar asked.

"No, it's for George and Nola and the baby," Kevin said.

"That's sweet," Pilar said. "I have to admit having him around has made living there a lot more exciting."

"I know. It's fun being an uncle," Kevin replied.

Pilar smiled. She loved watching Kevin take care of Nicholas. It reinforced her idea that one day Kevin would make an amazing father. She was lost in that thought, thinking about their future as parents one day. She couldn't wait for the day to arrive, but first she had to finish her master's program, which made her remember—

"Oh shoot. Stop," Pilar said as she slapped her hand on the door. Kevin pressed on the brakes.

"What?" he asked, afraid something was approaching from behind that he didn't see.

"I forgot my dry cleaning," Pilar said. "And I need it for tomorrow's presentation." She had gotten so lost in her train of thought that she had forgotten about it.

"So, you want me to turn around?" Kevin asked. The dry cleaner was in the opposite direction.

"Would you mind?" Pilar asked sweetly.

"Actually, I would," Kevin replied.

"Really?" Pilar asked. She was thrown by Kevin's response. It wasn't that far out of the way. "But I need it," Pilar said thinking about how she still had two hours of editing to complete for the presentation.

"I know," Kevin said.

"But you're not going to help me?" Pilar asked.

"I am. In fact, I already picked it up for you. It's lying flat in the trunk. The guy said that'd be a better way for your dress to travel so it didn't wrinkle," Kevin said.

Pilar looked over at Kevin who was now grinning ear to ear.

"When did you do that?" Pilar asked with surprise.

"I told you, I got out early," Kevin replied.

"Yeah, but I never mentioned anything about it," Pilar said.

"No. But you left the claim check in the glove box and I saw the date and decided to go get it for you," Kevin said. "I figured you'd be stressed with the presentation coming up and I thought I'd help out."

"Wow. That's really thoughtful," Pilar said as she reached over and squeezed Kevin's hand. "Thank you."

"You're welcome," Kevin replied.

Pilar sat and took in the moment. She appreciated when Kevin did small acts like these—doing things not because she told him to but out of his own kindness and unselfishness. It made her feel loved and respected. She felt grateful that she had a husband who thought of her in all the unexpected ways.

"Hey, doesn't that look like the Coen brothers over there?" Pilar said as she peered out the window. Two men wearing glasses with bushy curly hair stood on the sidewalk in front of the local bakery. Kevin looked over as they waited at a red light.

"It kind of does. I guess it's possible," Kevin replied. "They are from here."

"Do you think they're shooting a movie?" Pilar asked.

Kevin was about to reply yes when he thought of something else. "Or do you think they're in town for another special reason?"

"No way," Pilar smiled.

"George was a pretty big producer back in L.A.," Kevin said. "She had a lot of connections."

"Seriously? Okay, but which one then?" Pilar asked.

"I guess that'll just have to remain a mystery," Kevin replied.

~~~

At the house, George was cleaning baby bottles while Nicholas napped in his bassinet and Nola slept in their bed. George was working hard to make sure that Nola didn't have to worry about the cleaning details so that she could focus on caring for Nicholas. She didn't mind the extra work and took pride in the fact that she could provide for her family in this way.

Just as she finished drying the last bottle, Nola appeared with Nicholas cradled in her arms. "That wasn't a long nap," George said as she walked over and gave each one a gentle kiss.

"Someone didn't want to sleep any longer," Nola said. "And it wasn't me."

Nola wiped her eyes as she made her way to one of the easy chairs in the living room. She sat down and prepared to nurse Nicholas.

"Can I get you anything?" George asked.

"A glass of water would be amazing," Nola said as Nicholas latched on.

She watched as George walked back to the kitchen. It was then that she noticed how much work George had done while she slept. Not only had George finished all the dishes, cleaned and disinfected the bottles, but there was also a basket on the counter filled with the baby's clean clothes and blankets.

When George returned, Nola thanked her for the water then asked her to sit with her. George eased herself into the chair next to hers and took a moment to relax. It felt good to be off of her feet for a moment. Nola turned her chair so that they were face to face.

"I want to tell you something," Nola began. "I see how much you've been doing around here to help with the baby and it really means a lot to me. I don't know how I could do this without you," Nola said.

"I appreciate you saying that," George replied. It felt good to be acknowledged for her efforts. Nola's kind and positive words had a profound impact. She reached over and placed her hand on top of Nola's. As Nicholas continued to feed, the two relaxed in each other's presence, appreciating the family they had built together. They spent ten minutes like this until Dr. Steve and Kulap walked in the front door.

"Anyone home?" Kulap asked in a loud whisper.

"We're back here," George replied.

Dr. Steve and Kulap walked through the kitchen and into the living room. "Oh, you like our chairs, don't you?" Kulap chided them.

"They're great," Nola replied. "Perfect for nursing and looking out at the lake."

"We like them too," Dr. Steve said.

"Here," George said as she got up from here seat, recognizing the hint. "Sit."

Kulap immediately sat down and lifted up her feet. "I'm exhausted," she said.

George and Nola exchanged looks *you're exhausted?* They then looked to Dr. Steve who simply shrugged his shoulders.

"What's everyone want for dinner?" he asked changing the subject.

"Steak sounds good to me," Kevin said as he walked into the kitchen catching the tail end of their conversation.

"Oh, hey, Kevin," Dr. Steve said. "You guys are home. It's gonna be the whole family tonight?"

"I guess so," Kulap added. "I suppose you need my help in the kitchen?" Dr. Steve nodded.

"Pilar and I can help too," Kevin said as Pilar entered. "Right, babe?"

Pilar nodded. "Of course," she said.

An hour later, they had all sat down to dinner when Kevin disappeared to his room. When he returned, he was carrying a wrapped package with a perfect little bow on it.

"This is for you guys," Kevin said as he handed George and Nola the present then took his seat at the table.

"What is this?" Nola asked.

"Just something for Nicholas," Kevin said.

Nola and George carefully unwrapped the box. Inside was a book, only it wasn't an ordinary children's book. It was a book written and created by Kevin.

"You did this?" Nola asked as she held up the book for everyone to see. Not only was it a beautifully illustrated book, but it also had built in puppets that the reader could insert their hand inside to control. Thus, bringing the book to life.

George placed her index and middle finger into one of the soft designs and the small puppet girl began to dance on the page.

"This is incredible," George said.

"Is this what you've been working on lately?" Pilar asked as she turned to her husband.

Kevin nodded with a smile.

"It's amazing," Dr. Steve said. "And incredibly thoughtful."

The whole Riley clan paid him compliments. For the first time in a long time, Kevin felt proud of his work.

"Wouldn't it be great if we all lived here forever?" he said.

Everyone turned to look at Kevin and shook their heads no. As much as they had learned to work together as one big family, no one was ready to commit to this situation for the long term, even though they still appreciated each other deeply.

"I think this deserves a toast," Dr. Steve began as he held up his glass. "To our growing family. A family that will always be there for one another through every change in life, every house move, every boat ride getting stuck on rocks, every race to the hospital to give birth. Here's to our future little Nicholases."

They all held up their glasses and clinked them against one another's. Kulap wrapped her arm around Dr. Steve's waist, looked up at him endearingly and said, "I'm so incredibly lucky to be married to you and to be a part of this amazing family!"

Dr. Steve humbly responded back, "No, I'm the fortunate one to have you. And so blessed to have all of you here with me."

Everyone raised their glasses a second time. The sound of glass touching glass reverberated with a special kind of love, a love that would serve as a constant reminder of healing and support as they moved forward in their journeys through life. As they encountered the challenges of the future that awaited them, the bedrock of this family bond would prove invaluable. With the support of one another they would overcome anything life handed them and successfully achieve their passions and most cherished goals.

Reader Note

If you're interested in diving deeper and learning more in detail how to improve your own romantic relationship or marriage using Dr. Steve Riley's principles check out the author's website at www.drtimmcccarthy.com for his transformational video courses and self-help couples coaching book:

Relationship Co-Coaching: A New Approach To Deeper Love, Less Conflict
by Timothy J. McCarthy, PhD

Or visit www.relationshipcocoaching.com for more learning.

About The Author

Tim McCarthy, PhD, is a Licensed Psychologist and Licensed Marriage & Family Therapist whose new approach—*Relationship Co-Coaching* has shown an 87% improvement rate of couples within the first 11 hours of therapy. Dr. McCarthy holds that society sets all of us up for problems by failing to provide sufficient relationship education. Subsequently, he is passionately dedicated to teaching the key *Best Practices* to achieve relationship transformation based upon his new approach and evidence-based research. His first book *Relationship Co-Coaching: A New Approach To Deeper Love, Less Conflict* (2015) offers a step-by-step self-help guide while *Life of Riley* adds a lively entertaining story for applying these principles in real life to solve universally encountered common relationship problems!

Visit the author website
http://www.relationshipcocoaching.com

www.ingramcontent.com/pod-product-compliance
Lightning Source LLC
Chambersburg PA
CBHW020236130626
46549CB00005B/1925